Would You Like To Be Jewish 2 ?

Dr. Akiva Gamliel Belk

- FOUNDER OF -

jewishpath.org • 7commands.com • bnti.us
B'nai Noach Torah Institute, LLC

Contact us at:
talk@bnti.us

Copyright © 2013
Dr. Akiva Gamliel Belk
All rights reserved
ISBN-13: 978-0615764801
ISBN -10: 0615764800

Publisher
B'nai Noach Torah Institute, LLC
Post Office Box 14
Cedar Hill, Missouri 63016
talk@bnti.us
First Edition 2013

DEDICATION

Lost And Reclaimed!

I was lost in a wilderness on a dark black cold heavy night,

There were no stars, no moon, no lights anywhere in sight.

My life felt unfulfilled and worthless. My peril was doom. Where was I in this blackness of night?

I was in jeopardy, insecure and uncertain of life's direction. Should I go left or right?

Who could I turn to? Where could I go? Who would understand my plight?

Where would I find an individual that has shared this lonely cold heavy night?

Who would understand the ardent desire of one lost '<u>nothing</u>' trying to find a path to reunite?

I have sought this path in tears plenty, crawling on hand and knee, searching for what is right.

Is there anyone out there? Help? Oh God, I need someone to show me this path of light.

Oh God, generations of my family have been lost in the gloom of this lonely cold heavy night.

Will it ever end? Will I find my way out of this wilderness of gloom? Will I find the Light?

No matter how impossible and dark the night there is always a way for that spark to ignite.

Feeling lost? Feeling alone? This book is dedicated to you. May God grant you light.

Would You Like To Be Jewish 2 ?

Table of Contents

DEDICATION..5
  Lost And Reclaimed!.......................................5
FORWARD..9
PREFACE..13
ACKNOWLEDGEMENTS.....................................17
INTRODUCTION..21
Chapter One...35
  Observances / Obligations..............................35
Chapter Two..39
  Feeling Rejected..39
Chapter Three..57
  Sabbath Is A Sign...57
Chapter Four...71
  Sabbath Is Holy To You!.................................71

Chapter Five	77
Guarding The Sabbath	77
Chapter Six	95
The Sabbath Draw	95
Chapter Seven	103
Sin	103
Chapter Eight	109
The Serpent	109
Chapter Nine	119
Angels	119
Chapter Ten	127
Repentance of Adam And Eve	127
Chapter Eleven	133
Cain's Failure's	133
Chapter Twelve	137
Offerings	137
ABOUT THE AUTHOR	151

FORWARD

Seems like everywhere I go I see signs, products with English and Spanish labels. I don't read or speak Spanish so as far as I am concerned it could be Greek or Latin – meaningless to me.

What's the point? When one is unfamiliar with a language – written or spoken they are at a great disadvantage. That is the way most English speaking readers are with the Torah, the first Five Books of the Bible, with the Tanach, the Torah, Prophets and Writings of the Holy Scriptures. Most English speaking readers rely on translators. These translators try to put what is phrases together to make what they see in Hebrew make sense to the English reader. Sometimes that works, sometimes it fails miserably. Then there are times when translators translate with a bit of bias. How is one to know if a word is being translated correctly? The only way to know for sure is to learn the language yourself. This is a daunting task for most of us.

The other alternative is to find someone you can trust who knows the language and ask them to translate a word or phrase. Dr. Akiva Gamliel translates a few words in this book that could change your life, make the foundation of your beliefs tremble and perhaps collapse or validate what you thought was true. Dr. Akiva Gamliel sheds light on the issues of Salvation, Sin, Repentance and many other issues. If you are a seeker of Truth this book will be a light on your path dispelling myths and untruths. This second volume continues to lay the facts out about a word that we all know but have never been taught the Truth on – Salvation. What do we need to be saved from? If our name was written in the Book of Life why would we need salvation? What about blood sacrifices? Are they needed? Why do the Scriptures say that the animal sacrifices will again take place when the Third Temple is built? Is that because we need blood sacrifices? What is the point of grain sacrifices? Did Adam and Eve repair their relationship with God? How would we know the answer to that?

Shabbat – are you familiar with the word? Do you know what it means? Do you feel drawn to it like a magnet? What are the responsibilities of Shabbat and who can Observe them? Is it just lighting candles, baking challah and saying some prayers? For those who have been raised in an Observant home Shabbat is a way of life. For those returning to Judaism it can seem to be a lot to absorb and learn. For those who are not Jewish it can seem puzzling.

Answers are found by seekers of Truth. Answers can be earth shattering or life altering.

Dr. Akiva Gamliel in his gentle but truthful way provides us with answers to many questions that for most are of major concern in our lives. We want to live for God – but how is that done? We want to be righteous – but what does that mean? We want to go to heaven when we die – but how is that accomplished?

Come walk with me through the pages of this book and you will find the answers you seek.

I am married to this wonderful and sometimes challenging man, [Kaw Naw Nah Haw Raw]. He sits at his computer for hours at a time writing. I often would prefer that he WALK AWAY FROM THE COMPUTER and help me around the house. However, I know he is doing what God Wants him to do. I need to try to organize my time better so I can study and read more. I think we all want to be able to have the drive that my husband has to study, pray and write about God.

I pray the Creator of the Universe will Bless all who read this book. May He Shine His light on your mind and soul to know and absorb the Truth.

Rebbetzin Revi Belk

PREFACE

Dear Reader this is the second Book of a series that I intend to do if our Creator is Willing. My intent was to take subjects of discomfort between Judaism and other religions and to discuss these with readers. Sometimes, it helps to put sensitive issues in writing. It also helps to give some background and supply references. When I quote a reference check it out. See if it backs up what is written.

The subjects we explore are INTENDED to CHALLENGE! My oldest son taught me something about challenging ones self.

Joshua entered the military at a young age. He made something out of himself. It was not easy for him leaving home as a teen. One day his recruiter phoned. He said, Mr. Belk your son Joshua asked me to phone. He wants to join the US Air Force. He is under age. His mother has already signed the papers will you sign the papers also? I inquired about what the Air Force would do for my son. The recruiter assured me they would send Joshua to the schools they promised. In short order Joshua was on his way to boot camp then later to several schools then overseas. Joshua served bravely in a war for America like Revi's son Anthony. We are proud of our children. We are a family of veterans.

Joshua had a goal all his life. It was a very high goal. I cannot share it with you. Yet, I can say, Joshua reached his goal. Then he set new goals.

When Joshua returned from serving overseas he put himself through college. He earned his B.A. Then Joshua, like his Dad continued on to post grad studies. Joshua earned his Masters. I am so proud of him. Then Joshua became an officer in the United States Navy. Oh boy, did that make me proud. I am a U S Navy veteran.

Dear Reader, I study with dedication. Joshua studied with dedication. When he phoned we would discuss his studies and how challenging it was to work, help raise a family and go to school. In the first Book I wrote 'There are times I have lost track of days and nights... Why? I want to know the Truth. Knowing the Truth comes at a cost. Are you dedicated? I have written the first book and this book hoping to reach out to those trying to find their way through the maze of religion. It is a struggle to know the Truth. What Truth am I referring to? The fact is, we discover what we think is the Truth today. Later, if we are open, our Truth may change and certainly grow.

Sharing in both Books has been my pleasure. Please feel free to visit at Talk@bnti.us

ACKNOWLEDGEMENTS

There have been some very great individuals who have had a part in shaping my life. I am very grateful to each of them. Who made the greatest contribution to my life? Only God knows. Who had the greatest influence on me? Only God knows.

I have been so blessed to be around men of vision. It would not be possible to name each. However, I would like to share about a Rabbi of very great vision.

It was the summer of 1993. My phone began to ring. I answered the phone. The caller was Rabbi Yitzchok Wasserman, Roshei of Yeshiva Toras Chaim in Denver, Colorado. He asked, 'Are you busy?

I answered, 'No'.

He requested, 'Can you meet me right away?'

I said, 'Yes!'

Rabbi Wasserman said, 'Akiva bring a tape measure, a clip board some paper and pencils and meet me at Hebrew Alliance just down the street from the Yeshiva.' I knew the building well. I attended services there some before returning to Judaism.

Immediately I drove to meet Rabbi Wasserman. He was in the main sanctuary when I arrived. He was walking between the seats near the front. It was like there was a glow on his face. He looked up. He raised his right arm and pointed at the building and said, 'We are going to buy this place.' There was a twinkle in his eye and a small smile on his face and the feeling of determination radiating from him about the size of a mountain.

I had the good fortune in seeing this goal reached.

Dear Reader, it is because of this man's vision and the vision of his childhood friend Rabbi Israel

Meir Kagan, Roshei of Yeshiva Toras Chaim in Denver, Colorado and other dedicated people that I am here. This is why I have the opportunity to write this book. Rabbi Wasserman and Rabbi Kagan are both graduates of Beth Medrash Govoha in Lakewood, New Jersey, founded by Roshei Yeshiva, Rabbi Aharon Kotler. They were joined by Rabbi Chaim Kahn in 1967 in founding Yeshiva Toras Chaim. They employed a young Rabbi with enthusiasm, vision and a love for his fellow Jew, Rabbi Yaakov Meyer who is now the head Rabbi of the Aish HaTorah Community in Greenwood Village Colorado. I am indebted to these great leaders for their love, patience, sacrifice, faithfulness, vision and instruction. I will forever be grateful for their help in my return to Judaism.

INTRODUCTION

This is the second book in a series entitled, Would You Like To Be Jewish. The back cover summarizes what book one discussed.

If you could be Jewish, would you like to be Jewish?

What do Jews believe? There are many ideas about what Jews believe. And there is a load of disinformation about what Jews believe. Teachers, Spiritual Leaders, Pastors, Priests and over 700 different religions all have ideas about what Jews believe. With all this speculation, how is one going to know what Jews believe?

Who do you think would be best qualified to share what Jews believe?

What if one's perception about Jewish Beliefs changed? Would that have an outcome on one's desire to be Jewish? If new insights were provided about Jewish Observances would this make a difference? What if a few obstructions were removed, would this make a difference?

Each of these questions are a good reason to read the first book in this series. This second book is built upon the first.

Within the writings of this book I will use the term '*the Torah Portion of the Bible*'. It is important to understand what I am doing. My purpose is to remind the reader that the Torah is part of the Bible. I do not want to isolate the Torah from being a part of the Bible.

We will use a number of Jewish terms followed by a forward slash defining the Word used.

Aleph to Tav - [א ת] When I use the words 'from Aleph to Tav,' I mean 'from the first Letter of the Aleph Bet, the Letter Aleph [א] to the last Letter of the Aleph Bet, the Letter Tav [ת].' The Et represents being all inclusive from the beginning of one letter to the conclusion of another letter. *'The word Et is spelled Alef Tav,* *the first and last letters of the Hebrew alphabet. It therefore implies a transition from beginning to end. Rabbi Ishmael therefore states that its main purpose [in the instance he is referring to] is to indicate the transitive sense of the word "created."*

Rabbi Akiba, on the other hand replies that the very fact that Et contains the Alef Tav implies that it superimposes the entire alphabet between the subject verb and the predicated noun adding all things that pertain to that noun (Cf. Or Torah, Bereisheit). See The Bahir pp 108, 109

In book one I stated, *The Bible has many varying interpretations. We will examine some of these expositions and seek a greater clarity so you will know if you would like to be Jewish.*

I entitled Chapter Two 'Feeling Rejected' for a reason. It was to say, I understand. It was to also discuss many forms of feeling rejected. Readers will find a lot of answers in this chapter. I identify with individuals who feel rejected. Rejection sometimes is a sign. When one is rejected sometimes it is because the puzzle piece is in the wrong puzzle. The puzzle piece does not belong with that puzzle set. It belongs to another puzzle set. A Jew trying to follow the doctrines of another religion should feel out of place. The soul of an individual that stood at Mount Sinai should also feel out of place amongst another religion.

We discuss rejection brought on by divorce when one parent is Jewish and the other is not. Children are torn between two parents that love them very much but believe differently. Book One is especially helpful with this form of rejection.

In Chapter Three we learn that one can know God without religion. Abraham knew God without religion. We learn a foundational concept. God Exists. He Exists -- unbounded by time Is His Existence. We also learn that religion attempts to compete with God.

When people got together in large groups what did they do? They formed religions. What do religious leaders do? They lead the people astray. They teach the people disinformation. What was the result? People rebelled against

God. God does not require non-Jews to gather in churches or Temples etc. Where does one read that God instructed these some 730 plus religions to purchase costly land and to build magnificent buildings? God requires non-Jews to acknowledge that Sabbath exists and that God exists.

Sabbath has a meaning. Sabbath is intended to be a delight. Jews enjoy Sabbath candles... Sabbath table... Sabbath Kiddush, i.e. Challah and wine... Sabbath songs... Sabbath stories... Sabbath prayer... Sabbath learning... Sabbath walks... Sabbath nap... Why? God Commanded <u>ONLY</u> the Children of Israel to Observe Sabbath. This means Sabbath Observance has two forms. The Children of Israel must Observe Sabbath as God Requires. The rest of the world is not obligated to Observe Sabbath even though elements of Sabbath are a major attraction.
Sabbath is a sign. Sabbath has a important purpose that SUNDAY DOES NOT HAVE! Sunday is named after a pagan idol. What religion named the days of the week after pagan

idols?

In Chapter Four we discuss the Observance of Sabbath. I write, *'Dear one, no matter what ANYONE says, there is only one kind of Jew. Being Jewish is a way of living. We have Observances to follow. When we follow these Observances we, through our actions, separate the Seventh Day from the other six days of the week. We separate ourselves from the rest of the world by the Observances we follow.'*

There are 248 Performative Observances. The number 248 corresponds to the 248 organs and limbs of our body. We are to use our body to perform good deeds. There are 365 Prohibitive Observances. The number 365 corresponds to the 365 days of the solar calendar. We are reminded not to sin everyday!

Chapter Five begins with our intent. The Rabbium say, 'Dress Jewishly and you will eventually reach that level.' Often that is true, however, we must focus less on looks and more on reality. Do you want a chocolate coated outside with nothing in the center? Do you want to be an 'all show and no go' type of Jew? Do you want to look kosher? Do you want to look frum? Do you want to possess Yiddishkeit? Do you want to look like you Observe Sabbath or do you want to Observe Sabbath?

Holy Reader, our goal as Jews should be... to be saturated with righteousness and not just chocolate covered righteousness. To be possessors and proclaimers NOT pretenders. Then our life will be a blessing to those around us AND THEY WILL KNOW IT!!

At a low place in my life years later the owner of the Kosher deli and I shared a few conversations together. He reached the goal. He was now Shomer Sabbath. I, his former mentor was struggling... I had been knocked off my penicle of observance. Reader, Jews do stumble. Remember What I said earlier? Don't judge Judaism by Jews! That is right! I have fallen. I have stumbled! Thank God I have also risen again.

Proverbs 24.16
'For a righteous man falls seven times, and rises up again...'

Chapter Six concludes with another reason why individuals are drawn to Judaism. Is it a mistake for one to feel emotion for Sabbath? Is it wrong to deeply desire to share a part of Sabbath Delight? Why can't I light Sabbath candles and say a blessing over Wine and Bread? I want to hug my children and grandchildren and to give them a blessing around the Sabbath Table.

Something special happens every Sabbath. A soul in Heaven unites with a soul on earth. In these four chapters we have written about the experience one can see. This is an experience one feels. Love and Joy for Sabbath is heightened when Jews who Observe Sabbath receive a second soul. The additional soul lifts ones being and helps to refresh us. The heightened experience of Sabbath is extended sometimes with a Malava Malka celebration. This is when Jews gather to celebrate the Sabbath Queen after Sabbath has ended with the intention of extending the Sabbath just a little longer. This is often done with good food, drink, music and much happiness.

There are many excellent reasons to be drawn to Sabbath. If you sincerely convert to Judaism you will begin a journey of rich, deep Spiritual travels. Again, this sounds like I am promoting Judaism. Not So! Not everyone can be Jewish. Again, only the souls that stood at Mount Sinai and received the Torah will be Jewish. The point is not to say I have it but you may not have it. The point is to explain why it may not happen. The point is to say that no matter how much anyone encouraged you to convert to Judaism it will only happen if your soul stood at Mount Sinai to receive the Torah. And if this is the situation, God has other plans for such a dedicated individual. Remember, 'He Carefully Examines and Knows our hidden most secrets; He Perceives a matter's outcome at its origin.' And it is His Will that is important, not ours.

In Chapter Seven we discuss repentance. Repentance is not complicated. God has Made a provision for each who sin. Forgiveness of sin has NOTHING to do with Jesus or priests. When one needs to repent from sin, all that is necessary is to take ownership of our sin, make a plan to not repeat our sin and to pay restitution for our sin then return to correct living.

In Chapter Eight we discuss the serpent. It is important for each of us to have an understanding of the serpent's role when Adam and Eve sinned. God Gave us His Observances to follow. God provided repentance for when we failed. We were allowed to operate freely within the bounds God Gave us. When we failed to follow His Observances this would result in sin. When we sinned we needed to take ownership of our sin, make a plan to not repeat our sin and to pay restitution for our sin then return to correct living. We also discuss why we have the power of choice. We have free will because we each have a good inclination and a bad inclination. How does this impacts us.

We learn that some religions depict the serpent / Hah Naw Chawsh as the devil... as a fallen angel... as a demon. None of these depictions are true. The serpent did evil and was punished for that evil. It begins and ends there. The serpent lied about what God Said and Intended. The serpent deceived Eve. The serpent cannot walk, talk or hear any longer. So our concern should be about our own evil inclination.

The serpent is a beast of the field end of story. We show in the original text that the serpent was not supernatural. We show how the serpent has been reduced to the lowest form of life with no hearing, no communication and being unable to walk like in the past.

In Chapter Nine we discuss Suton, the Angel God assigns to test us. God wants us to succeed. Suton prays for us while we are being tested that we will succeed. We also review the fallen angels Shamchazai and Azael who caused many sins and were destroyed.

We are all subject to the tests of our own Yetzer Raw in conjunction with Suton, it is just as easy for us to pass a test as it is to fail a test. The same effort is required to succeed as to fail. God's Intention is for us to be successful! We have all the tools to be successful! No person is created or born with a greater advantage. God is Fair! God is Just! So, dear ones, be encouraged with your potential for success. Do not fear Suton or your Yetzer Raw. Scale the mountain! Be successful! Be happy! Do not fear the descriptions other religions paint of the Suton's power to destroy. Do not be fearful from their claims and threats of hellfire and damnation. God loves us! Love God! Love each other! Accept tests in their proper perspective! Succeed!

In Chapter Ten we discuss how Adam and Eve repented. What sin / sins did they commit? How do we know Adam and Eve returned to a proper relationship with God? Do we actually need to define Adam and Eve's sins or is it sufficient enough to say they sinned. They confessed their sins. Our Creator required restitution and they each returned to a proper relationship with our Creator. It's that simple. **God Makes the path of return easy.**

Chapter Eleven discusses our attitude. Is our attitude wholesome, righteous, pure and honest or is it flawed? There are many ways to give our Creator less than the best and from the back instead of the front so to speak. What do we do? Do we give from the best or the worst? What is the attitude of our heart? Do we desire to honor our Creator with the best or do we try to pawn off our junk and discards to our Creator?

Chapter One

Observances / Obligations

Dear Reader, the following thirteen Principles are concepts. Our approach to the question of *Would You Like To Be Jewish* is from conceptual base rather than a list of observances. We review the broader picture. We learn the concept before we learn the specifics. So, we are providing a list of thirteen concepts that we will draw upon in discussions throughout this book.

- Praised and Exalted Is the Living God -

1.) He Exists -- unbounded by time Is His Existence.

2.) He Is One -- and there is no unity like His Oneness. His Oneness Is Incomprehensible and Infinite.

3.) He has no semblance of a body. He does not

have physical form. There is no comparison to His Holiness.

4.) He Preceded every being that was created -- He Is the First. Nothing precedes His Precedence.

5.) He Is the Master of the Universe to every creature. He Manifests His Greatness and His Supremacy.

6.) He Gave His Prophecies to His treasured splendrous people.

7.) In Israel none like Moses arose again. He is a prophet who clearly perceived His Vision.

8.) God Gave the Torah of Truth through His Prophet, the most trusted of His household, containing the 613 Precepts of the Bible to His People. Everyone has an obligation to Observe certain precepts.

9.) God Will Never amend nor exchange His

10.) He Carefully Examines and Knows our hidden most secrets; He Perceives a matter's outcome at its origin.

11.) He Rewards man with Kindness according to his deed; He Places evil on the wicked according to his wickedness.

12.) By the End of Days He Will Send our Messiah, to redeem those longing for His Final Salvation.

13.) God Will Revive the dead in His Abundant Kindness -- Blessed is His Praised Name forever.

SUMMARY – The Thirteen Concepts Teach belief in God, The legitimacy of *The Torah Portion of the Bible*, human responsibility and our rewards for obedience.

Chapter Two

Feeling Rejected

10.) He Carefully Examines and Knows our hidden most secrets; He Perceives a matter's outcome at its origin.

Psalms 55.6-9.
Fearfulness and trembling have come upon me, and horror has overwhelmed me. And I said, Oh that I had wings like a dove! For then I would fly away, and be at rest. Behold, then I would wander far off, and remain in the wilderness. Selah. I would hasten to find a refuge from the windy storm and the tempest.

At the beginning of *Would You Like To Be Jewish* Book One I asked, Would you like to be Jewish? In Book One we had a perception of Judaism. A number of questions have now been cleared up. Have we accepted or rejected Judaism on what we thought it is to be Jewish? Our position was based on an incorrect perception about Judaism. Judaism has an attraction. The attraction is real. Those who read Book One and are continuing here have a strong attraction to Truth, fairness and accuracy. Your attraction may be because of a hunger to learn about Judaism or a growing desire to convert. If you are supposed to be Jewish then my goal is to help you succeed.

Christians portray Jesus as this friendly loving Jewish Rabbi who fights the established system, defends the widows and the poor, loves little children, heals the sick and much more. He suffers. He is beaten. He dies. Children grow up with this portrait of Jesus. Christians feel a closeness to Judaism because of their perception of Jesus. The nativity scene, the baby Jesus, Mary and Joseph, the star, the wise men and the angels publicize these ideas... these images... these feelings of emotion that for whatever reason just draws people to Judaism. Every year from the middle of November until the middle of January there is this unified promotion of peace and goodwill to all. The beauty of lights and snow and this friendly man with a white beard in a red suit... It's really quite wonderful.

How much fluff is there? Loads!

In Book One your desire to be Jewish was tested. Regardless of your reason for desiring to be Jewish I am beginning to think you are real. However, we must continue the filtering process. How does one really come to know if what they feel inside is real. Well, How do you feel about Book One? We discussed the 613 Observances. These Observances are the foundation of Judaism. So if you agree and are eager to begin learning and following each Observance with your entire being, then you should feel strengthened and be encouraged.

This brings us to the Tenth Concept.
10.) He Carefully Examines and Knows our hidden most secrets; He Perceives a matter's outcome at its origin.

Our lives are described as a flower that blooms in the morning and cut down in the afternoon. Our lives in measurement with eternity is like the flash of an eye. We are here in this universe that God Created, as humans for about one breath. Then we are gone. Wow! Yet even though we are tiny and miniscule we each are noticed by our Creator. Our Creator Carefully Examines and Knows our hidden most secrets. NOTHING is hidden from our Creator. Our Creator understands from top to bottom every side of our rejection. Even before our Name was recorded in the Book of Life our Creator Knew our purpose, our journey and our outcome from inception to completion.

Dear Reader, at this point in our discussion I am not concerned about what your beliefs are. That is entirely up to you. My concern is helping you develop into the individual God has Chosen you to be. My goal is to continue to help you find answers. My goal is to help you find what you are seeking.

Up to this point I have not been pumping

Judaism. I did not say one word about the beauty of each Command. Yet, there are many beauties. Are you one of the millions of individuals that need to find peace and true solace? Do you have a desire to break out of your present life? Are you miserable? Are you like King David? Are you seeking for a peace and a hope that seems to always be around the next bend, and the next bend? Do you feel like you just want to sprout wings and fly off to some lonesome peak away from it all? Do you feel out of place in your home, and like the black sheep among relatives? Is your Spiritual community a social entertainment center. Do you ask Teachers and Spiritual Leaders the kind of questions that can get a Saint excommunicated? Are you frustrated with the shallow non answers to your pertinent questions. Do you feel fed up with being told to just believe and to trust God for the answers. Do you keep snow shoeing forward hoping something good will happen. Well it has. You have this book. 'Would You Like To Be Jewish 2 ? Are you looking for that place to escape to? The place of escape is Sabbath. I cannot think of anything more beautiful or wonderful than Sabbath, Kaw Naw Nah Haw Raw!

Over a period of time you will receive answers.

Dear Reader, I know what this feels like. I understand what you are feeling. I have been there. I understand what it is like to have this tiny little light in one's soul that just keeps burning and burning and nothing feels good or fits until you begin studying Ha Torah. It is not difficult to describe what it is like when one comes home. When one returns to Torah Observances... when one returns to Judaism... when one experiences what their grandparents or great grandparents held so dear. The feeling is overwhelming, wonderful. Puzzle pieces come together. Things actually fit. For the first time in one's life one does not feel like a misfit.

I remember those sleepless nights when I tossed and turned, when I tried with all my being to find a way to make my religion work with Judaism. They were different. No matter how much I tried to make these two religions work together they don't because they are different. I struggled with this for years. I was tormented by those differences for years. I could not let Christianity go because I believed in Jesus. I believed Jesus was the Messiah. I believed Jesus was the son of God. I believed Jesus was God. This is a VERY DIFFICULT PLACE TO BE!! I needed answers. There was no one who could help me. There was not one I could talk with that could provide me with answers. It was an awful time. I hung between being married to a nice Christian lady and my need to return to Judaism. I could not return to Judaism because of my Christian beliefs. I was stuck! Do you feel stuck? I encourage you to pick up a copy of my book Entitled: *A Sincere Journey Ends Without Jesus*. The book is easy to read. You will identify with Chapter One, The Jewish Soul Cries Out and Chapter Two The Struggle.

Listen! There are many wonderful Christian people. They are not Jewish. They do not have this dilemma. They have no reason to think about the things I think about or the things you may be thinking about.. All my life I was different. This is how it is for an individual who is OUT OF THEIR ELEMENT!

Here is what happened for me. Over what seemed like eternity, maybe three years I began to see the pieces of the puzzle fit together. I had to erase some of what I learned. It was necessary to go back and research everything I considered significant about my beliefs from the ground up. The Truth stands tall - lies fall!

As Dean of Jewish Studies at B'nai Noach Torah Institute, LLC I am very firm about references as some of you already know. As I began my return to Judaism one very important lesson was REFERENCE EVERYTHING!! Solomon said, *'There is nothing new under the sun,* Ecclesiastes 1.9. This means someone, somewhere has discussed it. Review what they wrote. Study it.

Dear Reader, there are somethings one MUST know for themselves. Translations are unreliable.

I own many. I began teaching myself Hebrew. I began translating Scripture. It was very difficult at first. However, the reward is this deep deep satisfaction that I can know what the Hebrew Scriptures really say. I encourage EVERYONE to learn Hebrew. Individuals write to me asking me to translate a passage. I am not a translating service. Many times a timely response is not possible. One has to be very careful when translating.

I entitled this chapter 'Feeling Rejected' for a reason. It was to say, I understand. One has to eventually make a choice. By the time you finish reading these books the choice will be clear. Part of making that choice is understanding where one is at. In Book One we began a frame work that we will continue in this book. By now it should be clear that the answers we are seeking were not in our hand. Have you ever played Scrabble? It's a board game. Each player draws seven letters out of a bag. No peeking! The letters are hidden. After each player has drawn their letters the first player has the option to make a word by placing letters on the scrabble board. Have you played the game? How many times have you needed a special letter? That letter could help you win the game but you can't seem to draw it. Maybe someone else already has it? You don't know. In the same sort of way it may be that the answers one needs cannot be found where they are looking. ALL THE ANSWERS YOU SEEK ARE IN *THE TORAH portion of the Bible.* At this point in our studies it is safe to say that for things to straighten out and finally make sense it may violate some of the religious doctrines one has been taught and firmly believed in from childhood. It was that way for me. I was not immediately ready to release doctrines I held dear for almost forty years. The very fact that you are reading this book suggests that the answers you need do not appear to be within the boundaries of where you have been searching. Thus we move out of our comfort zone just a little. We test out the waters of what it might be like to be Jewish.

On one Sabbath in a Messianic Congregation I

received a beautiful revelation about Sabbath. The revelation was so powerful that it motivated me. Up until that time I worshipped on Sunday. For me Sunday was the Sabbath. However after this revelation I did some serious research. I phoned a Seventh Day Baptist Pastor and sought counsel. I also phoned a Seventh Day Adventist Bookstore and sought assistance. I remembered an airplane flight some twenty plus years before. I sat next to a Seventh Day Adventist man during the flight. He shared with me about the Seventh Day. In Bible College One of the Professors was an Adventist. Her and her husband invited us to visit one Friday evening. They shared with me and my wife about honoring the Seventh day. Then there was a lady who attended my father's congregation, Bethel Temple. She was an Adventist. I remember my parents discussing their concerns about her. They were concerned she would become a problem. As I recall we were warned not to go around her. No phone calls. No visits etc. Stay away from her.

I was raised as a Christian but at the age of

thirty-nine began my return to Judaism. I was born Jewish. If you have a Jewish mother you are born Jewish regardless of your father. With DNA today one can prove who there father is. If one's father is Jewish then they should also be Jewish. But that is not exactly how it works. This maybe frustrating and seem ridiculous yet we must follow the directions of our Sages. Sometimes this causes a lot of pain. I understand that pain. Neither of my sons are Jewish. When my sons were born I was married to a nice Christian lady. She is a good mother. Dear Ones, this is the penalty of sin. I sinned by marrying outside of Judaism and must face the consequences of my actions. I deeply love our sons and wish only the best for them. Yet, I understand, they are not Jewish and I represent a challenge to their way of life. They have done nothing wrong yet, they suffer because of me.

If your father is Jewish and your mother is not, I ask you to think of it like this. Judaism is black and white. That is good. You always know where you stand. If you want to be Jewish do the conversion. Don't convert because your father wants you to or because of family pressure. Convert because you agree with Judaism.

Fathers, it is a big mistake to pressure our children to convert no matter how deeply we want or need them to convert. If the soul of our children did not stand at Mount Sinai we are only hurting them and ruining our relationship with them. We cannot make them what they cannot be. I am sobbing as I type these words. I have been the source of much hurt to my sons. They have little to do with me. It is their choice. I respect it. I also understand, I helped to re-enforce their decisions. My actions pushed my sons away. I want them to be good men, to love God, to be good husband and fathers, and to Observe the Torah Portion of the Bible that our Creator requires everyone to follow. It is not difficult!

Children, only you know how difficult it is when parents divorce. It can be much more difficult when one parent is Jewish and the other is not. If you have a father like me who has tried to pressure you to convert to Judaism, I understand it is very unpleasant. It is uncomfortable to be around him. There can be constant hassles. It does not make for a good loving relationship with your father. Yet, REGARDLESS of how difficult your father is you do have responsibilities to honor your father. And you must do this by calling him some, by visiting him some, by remembering his birthday etc. I am saying it is necessary to forgive your father and to be bigger than your father.

There is another group - divorce is very challenging too. Children who are born of a Jewish mother but whose father is not Jewish. You are Jewish and are accountable to God for your actions. God requires you to live and act as a righteous son or daughter of Israel. You may not like it but this is what God Expects. There are situations where Jewish children are placed with a non-Jewish father or relative. This is a very challenging arrangement. One should obey their parent / relative providing their requests are legal.

Then, later when you are on your own you should begin the process of returning to Judaism. In this chapter we are discussing many forms of feeling rejected.

I must be candid. *The Torah portion of the Bible* Teaches that our sins can have deep roots even to the fourth generation.

Exodus 34.7
Keeping mercy for thousands, forgiving iniquity and transgression and sin, and that will by no means clear the guilty; visiting the iniquity of the fathers upon the children, and upon the children's children, to the third and to the fourth generation.
The serpent sinned 5,773 years ago. The serpent has been crawling on the ground ever since. Eve sinned. From that day women experience pain in child birth. Adam sinned. The ground is still producing weeds. The climate in our world was forever changed with the destruction of those in the flood. Dear reader sin has consequences that can have a very far reaching impact.

We cannot go back and reverse our sins. We cannot change the feelings of rejection we caused or that we have received. What we can do is to follow our Creators Observances. When each of us follows our Creators Observances over time we all will return to a road of peace and tranquility. Sin will have passed through our world. Sin will be gone and eventually the traces of sin will also be gone

.

We must ask the question again, What does God Want? What does God Require?

SUMMARY - The pieces of the puzzle should be beginning to fit together. The Mount Sinai experience has passed. Either we were or were not there. We cannot change that. At this point some who are reading this book know their souls were not at Mount Sinai. Do your best to observe the Observances our Creator requires of you. Observing the Obligations will insure that you will go to heaven when your body dies and you will be happy.

If you know you are Jewish, i.e. born of a Jewish mother you have an important responsibility. It is necessary to learn more about your heritage and to do your best to observe the 613 Commands of Ha Torah. It would be good to seek the counsel of an Observant Rabbi. You simply tell the Rabbi how you know that you are Jewish and request his assistance. He will assist you.

Chapter Three

Sabbath Is A Sign

Concept One is God Exists.
1.) He Exists -- unbounded by time Is His Existence.

Exodus 31:13,14
And you, [Moses], speak [these Words] to the Children of Israel saying, Everything [from the Letter Aleph to the Letter Tav of] My Sabbath you, must observe, **for [Sabbath] is a sign** *between Me and yourselves [passed down] to each of your generations to know that I, The Lord, am making you Holy [Separated]. And you must observe everything [from Aleph to Tav of] Sabbath for it is Holy to you*

Dear Reader, did you know Sabbath is a 'SIGN'? How is Sabbath a sign? What makes Sabbath a sign?

Camping is one of the fun things families can enjoy together. One summer our family had the opportunity to share a weekend camping trip in the Colorado mountains. We left Denver on Thursday afternoon. This adventure was to an area above Georgetown.

On our way up the mountain we did not visit Georgetown or Idaho Springs. Our plan was to visit on our return to Denver, Sunday. Thursday evening was designated to find a proper campsite, gather wood, enjoy a campfire and to tell stories. Friday was set aside for relaxing and Sabbath preparation. It rained throughout most of the day on Friday. Still we gathered more wood for our pre-Erev campfire. We would build a large fire before Sabbath began, then after evening prayers, Kiddush and supper, we would sit around the campfire. We would stay up quite late since we couldn't put the fire out. It had to go out on its own. Yet it was a very enjoyable evening.

During the late afternoon Joel, my youngest son and I were practicing several Sabbath niggunim /

tunes at our campsite table when a young girl chased a chipmunk into our site. I thought, Why did that little girl do that? It really puzzled me... A little later she returned. She walked right up to our table and proudly announced, 'I'm Jewish.' She said, 'I heard you singing several Sabbath Songs.'
I asked her, 'What is your name?'
She said, 'Sarah.'
'How old are you, Sarah?'
She responded, 'Six.'
We talked for a few minutes when her distraught grandmother appeared. Needless to say, Grandma was not too happy to find Sarah talking with strangers. In a very nice way I agreed with Sarah's bubbie and invited the entire family for an Erev Sabbath meal. Later Sarah's father stopped by to affirm. That evening we enjoyed Sabbath with our guests at our mountain table around the campfire. We shared Torah, sang, laughed and had a pleasant evening.

Why do these things happen? I don't know! Only the Creator does.

Even in the mountains of Colorado high above the city of Georgetown in an out of the way camping area, God brings Jews together. Just as a little six year old girl made her connection to other Jews, to Erev Sabbath and to Sabbath, make your connection.

Dear Reader, Sabbath is a Sign. Sarah saw and heard the signs of Sabbath all around her. She saw my wife in a skirt with a head covering. She saw Joel and myself wearing Kippah's. She saw my Tzitzit's, the Sabbath Candlesticks, the challah board and knife, the kiddush cup . There were plenty of signs to identify Sabbath was approaching.

Let's try to connect with each other as Sarah did. Let's walk together in the same direction ... on the Jewish path.

Sabbath is supposed to be a sign. Yet, the only way that Sabbath is a sign is when the Children of Israel properly observe Sabbath. In other words, half of a stop sign is not a full stop sign. It may not accomplish what it is intended to do. In the same way, partial observance of Sabbath by the Jew does not fulfill the agreement in the Torah.

If you want to be Jewish, Sabbath must be at the center of one desire and at the top of one's desire. If one looks at Sabbath as a day they cannot go shopping... cannot play golf... cannot wash the car or mow the lawn then a problem exists.

Some religions teach Sunday is the day of rest. No where in the Bible does it say Sunday is the day of rest.

Exodus 20.8 – 11
Remember the Sabbath Day, to keep it Holy. Six days shall you labor, and do all your work; But the Seventh Day is the Sabbath of the Lord your God; in it you shall not do any work, you, nor your son, nor your daughter, your manservant, nor your maidservant, nor your cattle, nor your stranger that is within your gates; For in six days

the Lord Made heaven and earth, the sea, and all that is in them, and rested the Seventh Day; therefore the Lord Blessed the Sabbath Day, and made it Holy.

Exodus 31.17
Therefore the people of Israel shall keep the Sabbath, to observe the Sabbath throughout their generations, for an everlasting covenant. **<u>It is a sign between me and the people of Israel forever;</u>** *for in six days the Lord made Heaven and earth, and on the Seventh Day he rested, and was refreshed.*

Concept One is God Exists.
1.) He Exists -- unbounded by time Is His Existence.
2.)
Our actions are very important. Our actions support the Existence of God. This is based upon the Torah Command to the Children of Israel that says observing Sabbath is a sign forever. Why does The Torah Say, *Remember the Shabbat to Sanctify / Separate it?* It is

because the actions of Remembering, Observing and Guarding Shabbat are signs to the world. Our actions are required in the observance of Sabbath. The same holds true in the observance that God Exists! Our children, grandchildren, neighbors, community, etc. learn about God's Existence through our actions. The modest way we dress is a sign that God Exists. Our careful, thoughtful speech reflect that God Exists. The Blessings before and after a meal are examples reflecting that God Exists.

Fundamental to all Mitzvot of Ha Torah is the Mitzvah of Believing in God. Honoring Sabbath says we believe in God.

Delight is a word that describes every Sabbath. Isaiah 58.13 reminds us that Sabbath is a delight. Anyone desiring to be Jewish has to be drawn to Judaism through the delight of Sabbath. The question is easy. Is Sabbath a day where you cannot do things or is Sabbath a delight?

Is Sabbath a day one cannot go shopping...

cannot play golf... cannot wash the car or mow the yard? Or is Sabbath a delight?

God wants our Sabbath to be a delight. Sabbath candles... Sabbath table... Sabbath Kiddush, i.e. Challah and wine... Sabbath songs... Sabbath stories... Sabbath prayer... Sabbath learning... Sabbath walks... Sabbath nap... Shabbat visits with family and neighbors... are each an attraction.

Would you like to be Jewish? Where does Sabbath fit into one's life?

After Teaching on the internet for many years one point is extremely clear to me. Elements of Sabbath are a major attraction to individuals who are not Jewish. So it is possible to be attracted to Sabbath Observances or customs while not being attracted to Judaism. There is a big difference. And so we come to this fork in the road. Is one drawn to the atmosphere of the Friday night observance, the candle lighting, the Sabbath Table, the Sabbath Challah etc.? Do you want to know just about these Observances and Customs?

I can understand this. The basis for Sabbath is God ended His Creating and Rested on the Seventh Day. Neither Adam or Eve were Jewish yet they would have entered into Sabbath in the Garden instead of being evicted just before Sabbath began. Can we imagine the hunger Adam and Eve experienced? They were Created from the dust of the location where the Holy Altar would stand. They were placed in this beautiful Garden. Then they sinned and were expelled from the Garden. All of this happened on the sixth day of creation. Now they were outside of Gan Eden / the Garden of Eden. The Seventh Day was approaching and they were on the outside looking in. They loved the Garden. They missed the Garden. They were experiencing the impact of their sin. The point is that they enjoyed the Garden. They experienced the beauty of the Garden. They could not return to the Garden in this life even though they repented of their sins. Yet they were not cast away. In the next life they entered into the Garden.

To a degree Sabbath is like the Garden of Eden to one who is not Jewish or Observant. It's like being on the outside looking in. In Judaism we Teach that the wife lights the Sabbath candles. Eve extinguished the Sabbath lights. The Jewish wife rekindles the Sabbath lights. Rabbi A. Y. Kahan The Taryag Mitzvot (Brooklyn, N.Y. Keser Torah Publications 1987, 1988) p 347 **Sabbath has a meaning. Sabbath is a sign. Sabbath has an important purpose that SUNDAY DOES NOT HAVE!**

The logic goes like this. If Jesus is a false prophet he cannot be God, or the son of God or the Messiah. If Jesus lied based on Matthew 12:40 writings, then Jesus sinned. If the genealogies in Matthew 1 and Luke 3 prove Jesus does not meet the criteria for the prophecy's requirements of Messiah according to 2 Samuel 7.12-14 then Jesus cannot be who Christians claim him to be. PERIOD!!

In the Book entitled, A Sincere Journey Ends Without Jesus I discuss in detail the quote from Matthew 12:40.

Matthew 12:40
For as Jonas was three days and three nights in the whale's belly; so shall the Son of man be three days and three nights in the heart of the earth.

I explain that according to the Writings in Matthew 12:40 and Luke 23:54 Jesus is a false prophet. Matthew says Jesus made this prophecy. Luke confirms it did not happen. Therefore it is a false prophecy and a lie. It's that simple. In my book entitled, Would You like to be Jewish Book One I prove, based upon the genealogies of Jesus in Matthew 1 and Luke 3 that Jesus cannot be the prophesied Messiah according to 2 Samuel 7.12 – 14.

There are many flaws in the Christian Writings. It should be abundantly clear to anyone who reads Chapter Nine, Would You like to be Jewish Book

One. There are reasons why noted theologians and scholars admit the Christian Writings have more than 150,000 errors. I have no idea if Jesus rose from the dead or not. Jesus does not meet the criteria for Messiah. This is what Jews know! Jesus cannot forgive sin! Jesus is not even a prophet! When one comes to grips with these points as I eventually did, one will realize as I did, that Sunday has no purpose in comparison to Sabbath. Sunday is named after a pagan idol. What religion introduced the days of the week used in many calendars? What religion named the days of the week after pagan idols? Why would they use pagan names for the days of the week? Why would they begin a new day at midnight instead of sundown? According to *the Torah Portion of the Bible* a new day begins at sun down. See Genesis 1.5; 1.8; 1.13; 1.19; 1.23 and 1.31. The point is to sow confusion! The point is to make understanding the Bible difficult. God Said to Moses that the present day ends at sundown and a new day begins. Why change it? Every year is numbered from creation until what religion changed this? Why change this? 730

plus religions do so in their doctrines... Religions own billions of dollars worth of land. What is the point to this? Are religions building the tower of Bavel again? Where do we read that God instructed 730 plus religions to purchase costly land and to build magnificent buildings? The point is only one day is set aside as Blessed... as Sanctified... as Special... as Holy... as a Sign. That day is Sabbath. God intended for Adam and Eve to observe Sabbath. However God Commanded <u>ONLY</u> the Children of Israel to Observe Sabbath. This means Sabbath Observance has two forms. The Children of Israel must Observe Sabbath as God Requires. The rest of the world are not obligated to Observe Sabbath. So if you would like to be Jewish Sabbath Observance is a Must!

God does not require non-Jews to gather in churches or Temples etc. God requires non-Jews to acknowledge that Sabbath exists and that God exists. In fact God dispersed the people of the land. See Genesis 11- When people got together in large groups what did they do? They formed religions. What did religious leaders do? They led the people astray. They teach the people disinformation. What was the result? People rebelled against God.

SUMMARY - You can know God without religion. Later we will see that Abraham knew God without knowing a religion. Sabbath has a meaning. Sabbath is a sign. Sabbath has a important purpose that SUNDAY DOES NOT HAVE!

Chapter Four

Sabbath Is Holy To You!

Exodus 20.8-11
Remember [Everything from Aleph to Tav] of the Sabbath Day, to keep it Holy... Sanctified... Separated... Six Days shall you labour, and do all your work: **BUT** *the Seventh Day is the Sabbath of the Lord your God: in it you shall not do any work, you, nor your son, nor your daughter, your manservant, nor your maidservant, nor your cattle, nor your stranger that is within your gates: For in six days the Lord Made [everything from Aleph to Tav of the] Heaven and [everything from Aleph to Tav of the] Earth, [everything from Aleph to Tav of] the sea, and [everything from Aleph to Tav of] all that is in them, and Rested the Seventh Day: wherefore the Lord Blessed [everything from Aleph to Tav of] the Sabbath Day, and Sanctified it.*

As we enter Chapter Four the tone has changed

a little. We are at a point now where we must measure our dedication. I want to know, are you dedicated? Are you committed? Are you devoted? Are you focused? Will you follow instructions? We have reached a point where those who are Jewish must make a commitment. It is NOT AN OPTION this is an important Observance from The Lord God! Dear Reader, Jewish life is supposed to revolve around Sabbath.

One evening I stopped by the home of a lovely couple. One of them opened the door and invited me in. When they turned on the hallway light a Sabbath atmosphere engulfed me. You could say that I felt like a doughnut being dunked in my favorite coco. It was wonderful. The Sabbath Table was set. Everything was in it's special place. As I remember, the Sabbath Table was set with ornate silver candle holders with long twelve inch pure white tapered candles standing like flag poles high into the room. There was the silver kiddush plate and kiddush cup. Each were a handcrafted art piece. There was the Challah board and knife imported from Israel with a specially designed Challah cover. The crystal flower vase with a special Sabbath arrangement. The Sabbath table was set with the finest china and silverware. The napkins were hand crafted and pressed. The feeling of Sabbath was very, very powerful. They are examples of guarding the Sabbath.

My dear wife, Revi follows this same pattern, Kaw Naw Nah Hah Raw! The other night ago I was writing this book after dark. I took a break from writing just at the right time. Revi had just removed the Sabbath Challah. The Kitchen... dining... living room area and hallway were accented by the smell of fresh baked Challah loafs coming out of the oven. I walked over to view them. They were luscious. The Rebbetzin's homemade loafs looked like they were professionally baked. They were gorgeous! I got this strong Sabbath desire. I glanced over to the dining area to see Carrie bat Brachah Rivkah's Yahrzeit Candle glowing. There were three long stem red roses in a vase. The Sabbath Table was set with our best plates and silverware. Dear Reader, that does something to you. I commented to Revi about the Sabbath atmosphere. I felt in our home. It was exceptional, Kaw Naw Nah Haw Raw!

On one occasion a Jewish man was returning home from a long week of out of town appointments. It was the sixth day. It was late Friday afternoon. Traffic was difficult. It became clear the gentleman would not be able to make it home before Sabbath began. He pulled his vehicle over in a challenging part of town. He emptied all his pockets including his wallet, charge cards and a tidy sum of cash. He left his cell phone. He walked the remaining miles knowing he would not be able to soak his feet or take a shower. He placed his entire life in the Creator's hands including a considerable amount of wealth sitting in his vehicle on a street in a very rough area of town. Thank God everything turned out well.

We would call this man and his wife Shomer

Sabbath. It means They carefully guard all the Observances God Has Given the Children of Israel concerning Sabbath.

SUMMARY - Dear one, no matter what ANYONE says there is only one kind of Jew. Being Jewish is a way of living. We have Observances to follow. When we follow these Observances we, through our actions separate the Seventh Day from the other six days of the week. We separate ourselves from the rest of the world by the Observances we follow.

There are 248 Performative Observances. The number 248 corresponds to the 248 organs and limbs of our body. We are to use our body to perform good deeds. There are 365 Prohibitive Observances. The number 365 corresponds to the 365 days of the solar calendar. We are reminded not to sin everyday!

As one learns the 613 Observances and begins following them they begin walking on a path of righteousness and holiness. This should be all of our goals.

Are you prepared to Honor the Sabbath?

Chapter Five

Guarding The Sabbath

Shemot 31:16,17
'And they, the Children of Israel, shall guard [observe] everything [from Aleph to Tav] of the Sabbath to accomplish [Torah Observance for] everything [from Aleph to Tav regarding] the Sabbath to their [future] generations as an everlasting Covenant. Between Me and Between the Children of Israel [Sabbath] is an everlasting sign that in six days The Lord Made everything [from Aleph to Tav of] the Heavens and everything [from Aleph to Tav of] the earth and in Day Seven, [Sabbath], He [God] Abstained from work and Rested.'

A jewel as beautiful as Sabbath must be guarded. When we guard the Sabbath. We guard the Sabbath Commands. We do our very best to observe the Sabbath Commands. We elevate the Sabbath above all other days. Yet how we

Observe collectively as Jewish people can be quite different. There are different levels of Observances. We are a diverse group of people. We are a mixed bag... Some of us are goofy. Some of us act a little crazy. Who knows? Don't worry. Jews come in all shades and colors. We are dispersed throughout the world. Yet even though all this is true there is a correct way to way to live as a Jew.

As noted in Chapter Three Non-Jews are not Commanded by the Creator to Observe Sabbath. If a non-Jew takes on certain Sabbath Observances for three times or more then this action becomes like a vow to God. One should be very careful about breaking vows to God! Once a non-Jew begins Observances they will be held accountable to continue the Observances in their proper way. Again, I said, No matter what ANYONE says there is only one kind of Jew. That is an Observant Jew.

Observance is an obligation given ONLY to the Children of Israel. Observing the Mitzvah of

Sabbath is an essential element of the agreement we the Jewish people have with the Creator of the Universe.

If non-Jews disagree with Ha Torah's instructions regarding Sabbath Observance that is not our concern in this discussion or in any of the discussions of this book. I am saying it is not up for discussion! The Torah definition of Sabbath Observance remains exactly the same as the day The Lord God Gave them. It is not open to reinterpretation. There is no variance as to how Sabbath is to be Observed. Yet, there is. I understand that there are many who have some Observance of Sabbath.... who keep some part of Sabbath Observance. The position of this book is to explain what Ha Torah says, while at the same time understanding that one may not be in a position to observe every detail, etc... That is between you and the Creator.

At this point I would like to say that it is possible one may be of Jewish descent yet not be included in the Torah's meaning of the Children of

Israel. How can this be?

When Jews disobey Ha Torah by intermarriage with non-Jews, immediately Sabbath Observance is affected. The marriage is not recognized by God, the Giver of Ha Torah. Since the marriage is not recognized by God, other areas that are also not recognized. In a marriage where the husband is of Jewish descent and the wife is a non-Jew, the children are not considered Jewish by observant rabbium. In this situation it is possible not to be recognized as 'the Children of Israel' even though one is a descendant of Jewish heritage.

The reason that we must make this distinction is because the Creator's agreement regarding Sabbath observance is only with the Children of Israel.

Dear reader, I understand that YOU MAY BE THE VICTIM OF JEWISH ASSIMILATION! I am sorry! I also understand that you may be the VICTIM OF FALSE TEACHINGS regarding

Sabbath Observance or who constitutes the Children of Israel. Again, I am sorry! You are the after-product of what someone else did... Now you find yourself here reading this discussion of Observing the Holy Sabbath. It feels awful being in this situation. You have done nothing, yet your Jewish past may not be recognized for one reason or another or only certain groups within Judaism recognize you as being Jewish. You have only accepted what someone else taught you. You feel this incredible need to return to God as a Jew or as a non-Jew but more doors are closed than seem to open. You receive much rejection and little or no encouragement. In some situations you are looked down on. You may feel like dirt. It can even be much worse, God forbid! For this I am sorry. We realize that only the Lord knows one's heart. Only The Lord knows our intention. Only HaShem knows our desires. Only HaShem knows and understands our past, present and future.

One's desire to be Jewish cannot be a fad! Dear Reader, you may think that you want to be

Jewish... that you want to return to the religion of your relatives... AND that may be true. Yet, as we are beginning to show there is much more to being Jewish than a sincere desire. Converting to Judaism or returning to Judaism requires much!!
Have you noticed, I repeat myself? Judaism is a way of life. A major part of life is Sabbath. EVERYTHING leads to Sabbath. We call it Holy Sabbath because it is separated from the other days of the week. We do things different on the seventh day. Being born Jewish and living Jewish are woven together in the same cloth. What is one without the other? We Mystically observe the definition of the Children of Israel in the Gematria of the words the Children of Yisroel. The actual definition of the Children of Israel is Children of Yisroel. We also observe that 611 is the Gematria for the Words Ha Torah. This means that being descendants of Yaakov is not all there is to the definition of the Children of Israel. Mystically there is more. The descendant of Israel must also observe all of Ha Torah... all the words of Torah and all the letters of Torah.

The words the Children of Israel are found only seven times in the Book of Creation, Genesis. Why does the Children of Israel occur only seven times? One reason is because the Children of Israel represents Sabbath Observance. the Children of Israel represents that connection to the seventh day. Within the Letters of the Word Israel we find that the first Letter of each Patriarch and Matriarch combined together spell Israel.

ישראל

י Yud for Yitzchok and Yaakov
ש Shin for Sarah
ר Reish for Rivkah and Rachel
א Aleph for Avraham
ל Lamid for Leah

Dear Reader, our theme in this chapter has been to show the connection between the Children of Israel and Sabbath. Every High Holiday is a Sabbath so making this connection is very important!

Now to those that want to be Jewish the question is, what do we do with this information? How do we react to what we are learning?

It is my hope that this book even though it is a bit stern in places will encourage those who have that tiny little spark of Judaism within them to return to Judaism... to return to Ha Torah... to return to learning, to return to Sabbath observance... And for those souls that stood at Mount Sinai to receive the Torah my hope is that you will be encouraged to go forward with your learning and enter a conversion program.

The last letter of Vih Hay Shev {and return} is the letter ב Beit. The ב Bet informs us of the distance we must travel to return. The place of shuvah, the place of repentance and the place of sacrifice for our errors is the ב Beit. It is the Beit HaMikdosh, the Holy Temple in Jerusalem. Since our Holy Temple is destroyed, that means one must look within the inner ב Beit {house} of their being. One must take the time to get acquainted with the softness, with the stark quietness, with the stillness of their inner house. THIS REQUIRES CESSATION OF ALL ACTIVITIES. Take the time to shut the world out for a while! Take the time to seek the stillness within our own soul. Relax! Meditate. שוב Return / Shoov. Find and follow the inner light in the inner house of the neshama / the soul. It is that inner light that connects us with who we really are.

Sabbath is the time for cessation of work. Sabbath is the time for connecting with God! Sabbath is the exact time for meditation!!
שׁוּב – Shoov, means to return. The last Letter of שׁוּב is the Letter ב Beit

שָׁבַת – Sabbath, means to rest. The center Letter of שבת is the Letter ב Bet. The Letter ב Beit means House. One returns to the House to the Holy Temple. The Holy Temple is the center of rest... The center of completion... Today we do not have the Holy Temple but we still have Sabbath. We can return to Sabbath every seven days. We can be restored every seven days. We can be calmed every seven days.

Dear Reader, שבת Sabbath is the foundation for Judaism. שבת Sabbath is the base. If we remove the Letter ב Beit from שבת Sabbath we have the Letter Shin and the Letter ת Tav remaining. Together they spell שת Shawt means base or foundation. ש ב ת Sabbath is the base... is the foundation of Judaism.

When other religions attempt to convert the Jew, or attempt to persuade the Jew to not observe the 7th day, as required in the Torah, they in fact are encouraging that Jew to sin. God forbid! Don't do this! For the ones that are not Jewish, yet but feel this burning desire to become Jewish, if that desires is strong, you will become Jewish. Conversion to Judaism requires normally several years of dedicated study. There is much to being a descendant of the Children of Israel.

Among our many classmates, we have some classmates scattered throughout the world, in observant conversion programs doing observant conversions. And if it is God's will, they will complete the conversion process. So it can happen. It is possible that your neshama stood next to mine and next to other Yidden {Yiddish for Jews} at Har Sinai / Mount Sinai. It is possible that your neshamah received the 613 Commands from the Lord God. Remember what you promised?

Exodus 19.8.
'All that The Lord Has Spoken, [I] will do!' This means you committed to an Observant conversion. Nothing less will fulfill your promise.
Now this may sound like I encourage and promote conversion to Judaism. That is not true. What I have said is simply an acknowledgment that the possibility exists. If you are sincere about a conversion to Judaism, we may be able to help you with a conversion program. However, the actual conversion will be up to you following through and observing a Jewish way of life as directed by the Rav doing the conversion. Once your conversion is final then you are a part of the Children of Israel in the fullest sense and

meaning.

Late one evening the phone began ringing. I answered wondering, 'Who could be calling at this time?' It was the Hornosteipler Rebbe of Denver, Rabbi Mordecai Twerski. What an honor it was to receive a call from the Rav, anytime day or night! Our conversation was short. A kosher deli was opening in Boulder, Colorado. TRI - Sulom would direct the Kashrut program. The Rav requested that I be the deli's Mashgiach. This was a great responsibility, 22 plus employees, plus training an on site Mashgiach, long hours, a very long drive through 36 miles of Denver's worst traffic... Yet, It was a great honor to accept this challenge as a short term assignment.

The owner wanted a kosher deli in an area lacking commitment to Torah observance. The owner and the cooks were Jews in transition. They were struggling with their commitment to dedicated Torah Observance. I know how that feels. I have been there. This was a difficult assignment! On the one hand here were Jews deeply committed to a kosher deli and on the other they were struggling with Kashrut themselves. What a mix. What wonderful people... They created a beautiful atmosphere that Jews from all walks / levels of Judaism appreciated. Several evenings each week the deli served as a place for learning. Various Rabbium taught classes. Jews would link at the deli for a meal and Torah study constantly. There is no way to describe the feeling one would get from observing the many Jewish intersections crossing at this Boulder Deli. May HaShem Bless the Jews that shared these goals for their good intentions and their Torah accomplishments.

However, holy reader, there were obstacles. The greatest obstacle was motivating those I worked with to Torah Observance. Everyday it was like hitting a brick wall. I pondered, 'How can one commit to owning and operating a kosher deli without being committed fully to Torah observance?' That was an obstacle. I tried many approaches with little success to motivate those around me. I davened {prayed} at the deli three times each day. I learned there daily. On Fridays at the request of the owner and staff we prayed and learned together. Again they were very wonderful Jews who would not commit to complete observance. Dear Reader, I love these special people!

One Friday I got out an old pair of blue jeans, a cowboy hat, shirt and boots, my bandana, silver dollar belt buckle, etc. I wore them to the deli that day. EVERYONE WAS JUST SHOCKED! I walked up to the owner. His eyes were just simply popping out of his head. His face was red! I said in a western drawl, 'Avraham if I was sitting at a bus stop and told you that I was a Mashgiach that worked at a Jewish Kosher Deli would you believe me?'

He began to laugh with this smirky look on his face as he responded, 'NO!'

I informed Avraham I would be wearing this outfit all day instead of my normal frum attire. I questioned, 'How do you like that?' Well, needless to say he didn't care for the idea. He was paying for the services of an observant Mashgiach NOT A COWBOY! My frum appearance spoke volumes to every visitor. It broadcasted a message to every customer, 'THIS IS A KOSHER DELI!' If I dressed like a cowboy, most observant Jews wouldn't visit his deli. The rabbinical supervision would immediately come under question.

Holy Reader, this was my attempt to say, 'We can look kosher without being kosher.' I was saying to the ownership and staff, 'You can employ kashrut supervision but truthfully that won't work because kashrut has to be lived. Being kosher is a way of life!' I was saying, 'I cannot supervise the cowboy side of all of us.' I was saying you can own a kosher deli, you can manage a kosher deli BUT people will not take you seriously as a kosher deli unless you live kashrut!! My assignment was up shortly after that and I did not renew.

SUMMARY - Dear reader, the Rabbium say,

'Dress Jewishly and you will eventually reach that level.' Often that is true, however we must focus less on looks and more on reality. Do you want a chocolate coated outside with nothing in the center? Do you want to be an 'all show and no go' type of Jew? Do you want to look kosher? Do you want to look frum? Do you want to possess Yiddishkeit? Do you want to look like you Observe Sabbath or do you want to Observe Sabbath?

Holy Reader, our goal as Jews should be... to be saturated with righteousness and not just chocolate covered with righteousness. To be possessors and proclaimers NOT pretenders. Then our life will be a blessing to those around us AND THEY WILL KNOW IT!!

At a low place in my life years later the owner of the Kosher deli and I shared a few conversations together. He reached the goal. He was now Shomer Sabbath. I, his form mentor was struggling... I had been knocked off my penacle of observance. Reader, Jews do stumble.

Remember What I said earlier? Don't judge Judaism by Jews! That is right! I have fallen. I have stumbled! Thank God I have also risen again.

Proverbs 24.16
'For a righteous man falls seven times, and rises up again...'

Chapter Six

The Sabbath Draw

Isaiah 58.5.
And those who shall be of you shall rebuild the old ruins; you shall raise up the foundations of many generations; and you shall be called, The repairer of the breach, The restorer of paths to dwell in. If you restrain your foot because of the Sabbath, from pursuing your business on my Holy Day; and call the Sabbath a delight, the Holy Day of the Lord honorable; and shall honor it, not doing your own ways, nor pursuing your own business, nor speaking of vain matters; Then shall you delight yourself in the Lord; and I will cause you to ride upon the high places of the earth, and feed you with the heritage of Jacob your father; for the mouth of the Lord has spoken it.

It was the early hours of Sabbath Morning. I was at the Western Wall. Men were gathered in this huge circle holding hands and dancing while singing a hardy joyful melody of praise to God in beautiful harmony. It was a joyous time. The fresh morning air was charged with energy. Then I awoke. I was actually in bed in our home in Missouri. Wow! I was still very blessed, thank God. Kaw Naw Nah Hah Raw.

Dear reader, if a dream... if a vision... if an event... if a strange phenomenon... if a word... if a thought... or if a comment can dislodge us from our daily routine, if we are disrupted and captivated by that disruption, then something begins happening that can change our life forever.

For me it was simply reading these words from a prayer book on Sabbath morning:
Moses rejoiced in the gift of his portion: that You called him a faithful servant. A crown of splendor You placed on his head when he stood before You on Mount Sinai. He brought down two stone

tablets in his hand, on which is inscribed the observance of the Sabbath.

So it is written in Your Torah:
And the Children of Israel shall keep the Sabbath, to make the Sabbath an eternal Covenant for their generations. Between Me and the Children of Israel it is a sign forever that in six days Hashem made the heaven and the earth, and on the seventh day He Rested and was Refreshed.

You did not give it, Oh Lord our God to the nations of the land, nor did You make it the inheritance, our King of the worshippers of graven idols. And in its contentment the uncircumcised shall not abide - for to Israel, Your people, have You given it in love, to the seed of Yaakov, whom You have chosen. The people that sanctifies the Seventh Day- they shall all be satisfied and delighted from Your goodness. And the Seventh Day- You found favor in it and sanctified it! 'Most coveted of days,' You called it, a remembrance of the act of Creation.

Now dear reader when I read the words, *'You did not give it, Oh Lord our God to the nations of the land, nor did You make it the inheritance, our King of the worshippers of graven idols',* I realized that the fashion, the assimilated way, in which I was living did not have a landing deck, a receiving area for The Lord's Blessings. It was necessary for me to prepare that landing deck, that receiving area through Sabbath Observance. I realized that just as the non Jew could NOT enjoy, understand or abide within the parameters of Sabbath Observance the same was true for a Jew in their world. I began to realize that contentment comes from finding your place in life. Like a puzzle piece, each of us has this unique individual shape and place in life's BIG puzzle. That Sabbath, I began realizing mine... Thank God!

Dear reader if you feel like an individual that is a box in a world of circles I understand. If you feel like the shoe is always too tight, I understand. If you feel awkward. I understand. How is a Jew living outside of Judaism supposed to feel. It should feel strange. Still, whether or not an individual is Jewish not necessarily the issue. We know millions of unborn souls stood at Mount Sinai and agreed to take upon themselves all the Observances as taught by Moses our Teacher. Now if an individual is willing to go this route who am I to stop him or her? What is the point in turning this one away? Yet the practice is to turn away those that desire to convert because Judaism is not evangelical now. We were in Abraham's day but we are no longer supposed to be due to Rabbinic decree.

Dear Reader, I understand your torchered soul. You want to be Jewish without all this Rabbinical red tape and the pain and suffering that goes with it. I get it! You stand in innocent and purity before God and feel twisted, bent, and at times trampled on, deceived and very frustrated. However not everyone experiences this. Not everyone goes through painful experiences like these.

SUMMARY - Is it a mistake for one to feel emotion for Sabbath? Is it wrong to deeply desire to share a part of Sabbath Delight? Why can't I light Sabbath candles and say a blessing over Wine and Bread? I want to hug my children and grandchildren and to give them a blessing around the Sabbath Table.

As we conclude our discussion of these four chapters on Sabbath there is a reason. Something special happens every Sabbath. A soul in Heaven unites with a soul on earth. In these four chapters we have written about the experience one can see. This is an experience one feels. Love and Joy for Sabbath is heightened when Jews who Observe Sabbath receive a second soul. The additional soul lifts one's being and helps to refresh us. The heightened experience of Sabbath is extended sometimes with a Malava Malka celebration. This is when Jews gather to celebrate the Sabbath Queen after Sabbath has ended with the intention of extending the Sabbath just a little longer. This is often done with good food, drink, music and much happiness.

There are many excellent reasons to be drawn to Sabbath. If you sincerely convert to Judaism your life will begin a journey of rich deep Spiritual travels. Again, this sounds like I am promoting Judaism. Not So! Not everyone can be Jewish. Again, only the souls that stood at Mount Sinai and received the Torah will be Jewish. The point is not to say I have it but you may not have it. The point is to explain why it may not happen. The point is to say that no matter how much anyone encouraged you to convert to Judaism it will only happen if your soul stood at Mount Sinai to receive the Torah. And if this is the situation, God has other plans for such a dedicated individual. Remember, 'He Carefully Examines and Knows our hidden most secrets; He Perceives a matter's outcome at its origin.' And it's His Will that is important, not ours.

Chapter Seven

Sin

The compassion of the Lord, the Mercy of the Lord and the Grace of the Lord is very great!! This is good! Our Sages Teach that God as the attribute of Justice Created everything until Man. When God Created Man He did so with the attribute of Grace, Mercy and Justice. *The Torah portion of the Bible says,*

Genesis 2.7

וַיִּיצֶר יְהֹוָה אֱלֹהִים אֶת־הָאָדָם עָפָר מִן הָאֲדָמָה וַיִּפַּח בְּאַפָּיו נִשְׁמַת חַיִּים וַיְהִי הָאָדָם לְנֶפֶשׁ חַיָּה:

And He, The Lord God Formed everything from the Letter Aleph to the Letter Tav of man from the dust of the ground...

The Name יְהֹוָה Lord indicates the attribute of Grace and Mercy. The Name אֱלֹהִים God indicates the attribute of Justice. Our Sages Teach our Creator did this because in His Divine Wisdom He knew man would sin and need much Grace and Mercy. At B'nai Noach Torah Institute LLC we teach a course entitled Bereisheit 104. This entire course is just about the enormous Grace, Mercy and Forgiveness of our Creator.

It is important to note that any time we discuss sin we must understand Grace, Mercy and Forgiveness. Our Sages Teach that repentance was created before the World was created, Pesachim 54a. What is Repentance? Repentance is for one to acknowledge his / her sin. This means we take ownership of our sin. Next we make a plan not to repeat our sin. Then we offer restitution for our sin. This means we offer to pay damages caused by our sin. When we do this we return to correct correct living. We have improved from when we stumbled. Our Spirituality is restored. We will look at two examples in the Bible. Adam and Eve and Cain.

We understand that God had a plan for humankind from before the beginning. God Gave us His Commands to follow. God Provided repentance for when we failed. We were allowed to operate freely within the bounds God Gave us. When we failed to follow His Directives this would result in sin. When we sinned we needed to take ownership of our sin, make a plan to not repeat our sin and to pay restitution for our sin then return to correct living.

Life has a bridge between man and God. The directions for building this bridge is Ha Torah. The bridge is constructed through observance of Torah! The bridge of Torah assists us in our transformation from a life of sin to a life of holiness.

In the chapter entitled Repentance of Adam And Eve, which follows later in this book, we share Biblical references and other resources that prove they repented. Little is said about the method of their repentance. Yet they repented. Based on so many religions making such a huge deal about repentance it is quite unique that *the Torah Portion of the Bible* says so little after Adam and Eve sinned and after Cain sinned. We should be asking why? **Repentance is important but it is SO OVER PLAYED by most religions.** In some religions, congregants have been hammered and hammered to the point that speaking about repentance has little affect. I think repentance and tithing / giving are so over done. Religions have ground people into fine dust. It is important to have a right relation with our Creator however that is up to the reader!! We will also discuss the repentance process in the chapter entitled Cain's Failure. It is very important to know how one returns to a right relationship with God. Before we do this we need to talk about how we were created with free choice and about the power of outside influences.

Shortly we are going to review Genesis 1.31 where our Creator Says at the conclusion of creation, 'it is very good'. This Verse speaks about creation but it speaks more about repentance from sin.

SUMMARY - Repentance is not complicated. God has Made a provision for each who sin. Forgiveness of sin has NOTHING to do with Jesus or priests. When one needs to repent from sin all that is necessary is to take ownership of our sin, make a plan to not repeat our sin and to pay restitution for our sin then return to correct living.

Chapter Eight

The Serpent

Our discussion begins with the examination of several Verses in Genesis. The purpose in doing this is to show the serpent was a beast of the field according to Genesis. There are several points about about the serpent we will note.

Genesis 3.1

וְהַנָּחָשׁ הָיָה עָרוּם מִכֹּל חַיַּת הַשָּׂדֶה אֲשֶׁר עָשָׂה יְהֹוָה אֱלֹהִים וַיֹּאמֶר אֶל־הָאִשָּׁה אַף כִּי־אָמַר אֱלֹהִים לֹא תֹאכְלוּ מִכֹּל עֵץ הַגָּן :

And the serpent was more subtle *from every beast of the field* which The Lord God had made...

וַיִּצֶר יְהֹוָה אֱלֹהִים מִן־הָאֲדָמָה כָּל־חַיַּת הַשָּׂדֶה וְאֵת כָּל־עוֹף הַשָּׁמַיִם וַיָּבֵא אֶל־הָאָדָם לִרְאוֹת מַה־יִּקְרָא־לוֹ וְכֹל אֲשֶׁר יִקְרָא־לוֹ הָאָדָם נֶפֶשׁ חַיָּה הוּא שְׁמוֹ :

The Lord God Formed from the ground every beast of the field...

Study these words.
And the serpent – וְהַנָּחָשׁ
Vih Hah Naw Chawsh See Strong's Concordance No 5175

Genesis 3.1
From every Beast of the field - מִכֹּל חַיַּת הַשָּׂדֶה
Mee Kol - Chah Yaht - Hah Saw Deh

Genesis 2.19
Every Beast of the field - כָּל־חַיַּת הַשָּׂדֶה

Note Strong's Concordance No 2416 is referenced in Genesis 3.1 and Genesis 2.19 for beast. Also note that Strong's Concordance No 7704 is used in Genesis 3.1 and Genesis 2.19. Lets note the Words *'beast of the field...'*

In Genesis 2.19 we note *when the beast of the field was formed* the Words כָּל־חַיַּת הַשָּׂדֶה

were used. The words are the same as in Genesis 3.1 except for one Letter. I want the reader to see *the Torah portion of the Bible* is saying the serpent was a beast of the field. The serpent was formed out of the ground by God. How do we know this? In Genesis 3.1 The Torah portion of the Bible informs us that the serpent belongs to the 'beast family'. **The Bible is not assigning some super natural strength to the serpent.** The Bible Says the serpent was cunning / subtle. Being subtle does not make one supernatural. Being crafty or shrewd does not make one supernatural.

The beasts of the field each had mates. See Genesis 2.20. Where was the serpents mate? Adam and Chavah named the serpent and his mate נָחָשׁ serpent, i.e. meaning a snake or a serpent. Many Chapters later on in Ha Torah the Word נָחָשׁ is used by Yoseif for a cup used for divining. Still this does not change the facts. The serpent was formed from the ground.

Genesis 3 shares the first challenge to what God Commanded Adam and Eve. We read that this cunning subtle beast of the field challenges Eve to sin. Adam is right there listening to the entire conversation. He watches the entire event unfold. He stands by. As ruler of the world he stands by. As the High Priest to all living he stands by. As Adam, the husband of Eve, he stands by. We know what is about to happen. Eve is about to sin. And, we may wonder why Adam did not get involved. We have to ask, did Adam know what was going to happen. I don't think so! If Adam had known what was about to happen, would he have become involved. Should Adam have commanded the serpent to stop! Should Adam have spoken to Eve? Should Adam have used force to to prevent Eve from sinning?

We know from Genesis 2.15 that one of the purposes of Adam and Eve being placed in the Garden was to Guard it. The serpent presented some safety concerns. Adam and Eve knew the nature of the serpent.

Genesis 2.15

וַיִּקַּח יְהוָה אֱלֹהִים אֶת־הָאָדָם
וַיַּנִּחֵהוּ בְגַן־עֵדֶן לְעָבְדָהּ **וּלְשָׁמְרָהּ** :

And the Lord God took the man, and put him into the Garden of Eden to cultivate it and to **guard it**.

We know the purpose of our Creator placing Adam and Eve in the garden was to guard it. Why did the Garden need a guard? They were the ones that gave the serpent it's name. They were not blind to the essence of the serpent as rulers over every living creature. Adam displayed his kingship by calling each living being. The act of calling displays Adam's superiority. When Adam called a creature, that creature was obliged to respond to his call. Dear ones, there is a great difference between calling and naming. The Torah states that whatever Adam Yeek Raw {called} each living creature then that became its Shi Mooh / name, Genesis 2:19. The Creator sealed each being with Adam's call / name. Dear Ones, this means Hah Naw Chawsh was inferior to Adam. This means that Hah Naw

Chawsh would report to Adam when Adam called. There is more to learn here than immediately meets the eye.

The serpent is called a beast of the field. The serpent is not on the intellectual level of Adam or Eve, yet, the serpent succeeds at persuading Eve to sin.

Dear reader Adam and Eve were created with a balance of power between their good inclination and their evil inclination. One was not greater than the other. Within each of us are the existence of these two forces. Both forces were created by God. This is how we know we have free will to choose. These forces are called the Yetzer Tov meaning, the good inclination and Yetzer Raw meaning, bad inclination. Simply put each of us, like a computer, has an original operating system with a Yetzer Tov and a Yetzer Raw. Both are equal. The function of the Yetzer Tov is to follow and to observe what God Has Commanded. The function of the Yetzer Raw is to challenge us to disobey God's

Commandments... The Yetzer Raw challenges our desire to love and honor God. The Yetzer Raw is not a demon or a devil.

The serpent was persuasive because he was connecting with their evil inclination. The evil inclination was being tried. The principle here is such an important factor to success. We meet people that we can influence. We can influence others with little effort to do what is right. When individuals are right where Adam and Eve were, they can be influenced even by a beast.

Listen! I have been influenced by our little shelty, Sarah, many times. When Sarah wants something she knows how to touch me. Out of no where Sarah will come over to me and nudge me with her nose. If I ignore Sarah she will repeat the action with more intensity until I respond. I can say no or find out what she wants. Sarah has caused me to get out of my office chair, walk down the hall to the kitchen, open the bread box on the counter and give her a piece of Challah. Sarah does not need to say a word. I get her message.

Any one of us can be influenced if it is at that time we are open to being influenced. This is what happened to Adam and to Eve. It's that simple! This is how a word of encouragement can have a powerful impact.

I know a Realtor that has a client who needs to sell her house. That's normal. However just about every time this Realtor phones his client she begins encouraging him. She understands the value of encouragement. She is using her talent to influence her realtor. Her husband, may he rest in peace, was a realtor. No doubt she encouraged him many times. What a blessing encouraging another can be. **Remember this Principle!**

We do not see Adam offering direction or encouragement to his wife. They were each taken off guard by the crafty words of the serpent.

Dear Reader, encouraging words are so powerful. Cutting and destructive words are also powerful. Recently a congregation leader shared an incident about an individual in his congregation. This was a mother and daughter incident. The daughter went to visit the mother for several weeks. The mother was so cutting while she was away. On one occasion the mother introduced her daughter to a friend. She said something to the effect, *This is my daughter. She is always causing me trouble.* The Congregation Leader reflected, *'Not only was the statement false it was hurtful.'* This is one reason why I Teach, choose words very carefully. Our words have impact on other individuals good and evil inclination. Please be very careful!

SUMMARY - God Gave us His Observances to follow. God provided repentance for when we failed. We were allowed to operate freely within the bounds God Gave us. When we failed to follow His Observances this would result in sin. When we sinned we needed to take ownership of our sin, make a plan to not repeat our sin and to pay restitution for our sin then return to correct living.

Some religions depict the serpent / Hah Naw Chawsh as the devil... as a fallen angel... as a demon. None of these depictions are true. The serpent did evil and was punished for that evil. It begins and ends there. The serpent lied about what God Said and Intended. The serpent deceived Eve. The serpent cannot walk, talk or hear any longer. So our concern should be about our own evil inclination.

Chapter Nine

Angels

Dear ones, certain religions have created a huge fear of Satan. They picture Satan as the devil, as a demon and as the serpent in Gan Eden. These religious teachings depict Satan as evil. They claim that the conclusion of Satan and his followers will be eternal death... destruction and hellfire. This is religious doctrine. *The Torah portion of the Bible* does not Teach this. However, we will discuss this in a few paragraphs.

Dear Reader, think about the Words of The Lord God's to the serpent. *'Since you did this, you are cursed [beneath] all animals and beasts of the field...'* Genesis 3:14 The essence of this curse is not only the removal of the serpent's superiority over animal life but the removal of the ability to communicate... to think... to reason.. etc. with humankind.

Do not fear the serpent. The serpent cannot harm us as it harmed Adam and Eve. *The Torah portion of the Bible* clearly states that the serpent has been reduced to the lowest form of life. One MUST only fear the Creator!

Now, having said this we must understand that I am not saying we will not be tested. Even though the serpent has no power over us mystically we can see there will be tests. Each of us will be tested. Mystically we see this in the curse our Creator placed on the serpent. What was the curse? Adam and Eve were made of dust. Our Creator Said to the serpent,

Genesis 3.14
'...upon your belly shall you go, and dust shall you eat all the days of your life...'

This means that even though, the serpent now crawls... and the serpent cannot speak... and the serpent cannot have intellectual conversations with us the serpent is still crawling around through the dust of out lives and as a result we must be careful. We do not need to be afraid. We need to be careful!! We have everything we need to pass the test.

Dear, dear ones, God Created an Angel to test us. The Angel has an important responsibility. The Angel is called Suton / Satan. The purpose of Suton can be easily understood by the following two examples.

First, before a jet is approved to carry passengers it must be tested. It is not enough to accept the word of the engineers or the manufacturer regarding the safety or performance of the jet. The jet must pass a series of tests to prove its air worthiness. Nothing short of testing the commercial jet will suffice. As a result our government has designed a series of tests that each jet / each plane must pass before it is certified for passenger use. From the consumer's viewpoint testing is very good. We want to feel safe when we fly. The consumer supports strict airline standards. The consumer wants frequent checks. The consumer wants frequent tests...

Second, when one applies for employment one often sends a resume along with an employment application. What is the purpose of the resume and the application? It is to demonstrate one's qualifications to the potential employer. If the applicant's resume and application are accepted an interview is normally set. Sometimes a second and third interview are required. Why? Each are series of tests that determine one's ability.

Now, dear reader, religions do not question the purpose for testing jet airliners or potential employees. Why then don't religions make this connection in a person's daily life? Why do religions associate problems in the neighborhood, at school or on the job with Suton? Why do they teach that one must rebuke Suton?

Dear Reader, God Created Suton for the purpose of testing us. However, the test is intended to prove us. **The entire time Suton tests us he is praying to the Creator that we will succeed.** Suton is NOT some fallen, sinful angel. Suton is not going to burn in hell for fulfilling God's Directives. **Testing us is the responsibility of Suton.** There is a great difference here between the serpent / the snake / Hah Naw Chawsh of Genesis 3 and Suton which was created by God. The serpent was punished because the serpent did wrong. The serpent was intent on testing Adam and Chavah beyond reasonable limits. The serpent lied about the end result and the consequences. Suton abides within God's Directives.

Dear Reader, if one cheats on their income taxes there are penalties. If one steals there are penalties. If one does wrong there are penalties. The Suton knows and acknowledges these penalties. The Suton understands that there is a limit to the scope of testing. The Torah carries the highest requirements of integrity, honesty and truthfulness. Religious leaders and teachers. must be so careful not to misstate or misdirect our students, our colleagues. God exacts great penalty for knowingly misrepresenting what He has Said.

Angels are 'Messengers' of God. Angels carry the exact message word for word in the exact tone etc. that the Creator Spoke the Words. This is why one may have difficulty with Genesis18 and Genesis 22. The Angels talk exactly as God Spoke the Words. This is what a messenger does. Angels do not have free will.

Fallen angels are discussed in the Bible. They exist. In the days of Noach two angels Shamchazai and Azael were permitted to visit earth with the Creator's Sanction. The Creator Allowed them to have free will. The Midrash records the story of Shamchazai and Azael.

These two angels believed they could sanctify God's Name on earth greater than man could. The Creator permitted them to try to prove their claim knowing they would fail. They did fail. Yet they needed an even playing field where they could rise or fall on their own. The Torah records that the earth was destroyed because of them {Shamchazai and Azael}, Genesis 6:13. However 120 years were provided for anyone to repent. No one repented. Shamchazai and Azael and all the evil people of the earth were destroyed.

The nature of the Yetzer Raw is not to deny the penalties or the existence of limits. The nature of the Yetzer Raw is to disobey what God Has Commanded, knowing that it is wrong. Yet the Yetzer Raw is not fooled or surprised when penalties are required for sin. The Yetzer Raw understands limits and when the limits are exceeded.

The Suton presents the challenges for us to obey or to disobey. The challenges are presented skillfully yet within limits. Hah Naw Chawsh did not observe these limits. Remember all tests are on an even playing field. Again we are reminded that prior to the flood of Noach the hearts of men were continually evil, Genesis 6:5. So while we don't want to dwell on their destruction we must acknowledge the possibility for failure and the consequences of failure. The potential for failure must be real, otherwise the test would not be valid.

SUMMARY - We are all subject to the tests of our own Yetzer Raw in conjunction with Suton, it is just as easy for us to pass a test as it is to fail a test. The same effort is required to succeed as to fail. God's Intention is for us to be successful! We have all the tools to be successful! No person is created or born with a greater advantage. God is Fair! God is Just! So, Dear ones, be encouraged with your potential for success. Do not fear Suton or your Yetzer Raw. Scale the mountain! Be successful! Be happy! Do not fear the descriptions other religions paint of Suton's power to destroy. Do not be fearful from their claims and threats of hellfire and damnation. God loves us! Love God! Love each other! Accept tests in their proper perspective! Succeed!

Chapter Ten

Repentance of Adam And Eve

Do we know, what Command God Gave Adam and Eve? What did God Say to Adam and Eve? What sin / sins did they commit? What were the sins of Adam and Eve? Do we actually need to define Adam and Eve's sins or is it sufficient enough to say, they sinned. They confessed their sins. Our Creator required restitution and they each returned to a proper relationship with our Creator. It's that simple. God Makes the path of return easy.

How do we know Adam and Eve returned to a proper relationship with God?

Our Sages teach that the Lord God Created repentance before he Created the universe. We know repentance worked because The Torah Says, in Genesis 1.31 מְאֹד טוֹב Tov Mih Ood meaning '*Greatly Good or Extremely Good*!

Genesis 1.31
And God saw every thing that he had Made, and, behold, it was extremely good. And there was evening and there was morning, the sixth day.

Dear Ones, this was AFTER Adam and Eve sinned. It could not be very good if they had not repented. The Torah does not say a great deal about repentance, yet, we do see evidence of Adam and Eve's repentance beyond Genesis 1.31

Sefer Raziel Ha Malach says Adam prayed for three days after he and his wife sinned. Sepher Rezial Hemelach, The Book of the Angel Rezial, Edited and translated by Steve Savedow, Weiser Books, San Francisco, CA/ Newburyport, MA Book One Part 2 Page 5 - **This is the Prayer of Adam, the first man. Adam prayed 'Forgive me...' Then on the third day the Angel Raziel came to Adam to comfort him. Angel Raziel said to Adam, 'Your prayers have been accepted.'** Avraham Yaakov Finkel, Kabbalah (Southfield, Mi, Targum, Nanuet NY, Feldheim Publishers,

Genesis 4.25

וַיֵּדַע אָדָם עוֹד אֶת־אִשְׁתּוֹ וַתֵּלֶד בֵּן **וַתִּקְרָא**
אֶת־שְׁמוֹ שֵׁת כִּי שָׁת־לִי אֱלֹהִים זֶרַע אַחֵר
תַּחַת הֶבֶל כִּי הֲרָגוֹ קָיִן :

And Adam knew everything from Aleph to Tav of his wife again; and she bore a son, **and she called his name Seth;** *For God, Gave to me another seed in place of Abel, for Cain killed him.*

This verse reveals God as Judge. The Torah Says, 'God' Gave me another seed. Why is this important? The birth of Seth represents blessings to Eve and to the world. The blessing to Eve is that previous issues were worked out between her and her husband. They reunited. They came together. This resulted in the birth of a righteous son. Children are intended to be a blessing from God! Ha Torah is testifying of improvement between Adam and Eve's Spiritual condition. The Torah is indicating God's Blessing on their reuniting. This tells us their relationship with God was greatly improved. They brought forth a righteous child. The Name Shayt / Seth means foundation. Adam and Eve considered their son Seth to be the 'Foundation of the Spiritual World.' During 130 years Adam and Eve were separated Cain brought much evil into the world. Cain brought evil children into the world. At that time the world had little hope. It was necessary for Adam and Eve to have a righteous son so that the world would populate with good. Adam learned the importance of bringing good children into the world. Just as Adam had been born circumcised, [so was his son Seth] born circumcised, Rabbi Moses Weissman, The Midrash Says (Brooklyn, New York: Benei Yakov Publications 1980), p. 68.

'Adam saw that Abel was dead, Cain was cursed, and Cain's descendants had gone in evil ways. It was then, after 130 years that He '*knew his wife again* - after a separation of 130 years (Midrash) - to ensure that worthwhile forebears of mankind would be produced (Malbim). Rabbi Meir

Zlotowitz and Rabbi Nosson Scherman, <u>The Artscroll Tanach Series - Bereishis Vol. I(a)</u> (Brooklyn, New York: Mesorah Publications, Ltd. 3rd Impression, 1989), pp 163, 164

The birth of Seth began a new Spiritual line from Adam and Chavah. All of us are from this righteous line from Adam and Eve / Chavah that began with Seth. The righteous Line of Seth has maintained righteous people from 235 FC (From Creation).

Dear Reader, it is from this righteous line that the teachings of *the Torah portion of the Bible* were passed from Adam to Shet to Chanoch / Enoch to Noach to Shem (Malki Tzdek / King of Righteousness) to Avraham to Isaac to Jacob to Levi to Moses to Aharon, to Pinchas... Avraham Yaakov Finkel, <u>Kabbalah</u> (Southfield, Mi, Targum, Nanuet NY, Feldheim Publishers, 2002) p 26.

The Midrash Informs us that Adam transmitted the Noachide Laws to him along with the Heavenly Garments provided after their sins,

(Rabbi Moses Weissman, The Midrash Says (Brooklyn, New York: Benei Yakov Publications 1980), p. 69). This is what Ha Torah is Speaking of when we read Adam had a son in his image. Ha Torah is Saying Adam's image was righteous. His righteous image produced Seth. The Noachide Laws are Seven Obligations that all Non-Jews are required to Observe. These Obligations expand out to cover how all of us should live in peace and interact with each other in a harmonious fashion.

When Ha Torah Says, 'God Gave me another seed' is also the basis of transmigration of the soul. The soul of Abel became the soul of Seth.

SUMMARY – We see Adam and Eve repented. Each of us are descended from them. Our DNA leads back to Adam and Eve.

Chapter Eleven

Cain's Failure's

We learn about sin and repentance in Genesis Chapter Four. Cain was a farmer. He brought a grain offering. That is fine. God loves grain offerings. We are taught this often in *the Torah Portion of the Bible*. Matzah is ground wheat, barley, oats, rye or spelt with water added. It is a poor man's offering. Cain'[s offering was not rejected because it was produce. The issue with Cain's offering was, it was spoiled flax seed. Cain did not bring the best of his fields. He did not bring the first of his fruits. God was not Pleased with Cain's offering. On the other hand Abel brought the the best spun wool and goats hair. He brought the best cream and the best cheese. They were from the best crop from the first fruits of his flocks. God was greatly pleased with his offering.

Cain sinned. He did not offer God his best. Cain

did not offer God his first fruits. The Lord God Came to have a talk with Cain. The emphasis of the talk is upon improvement and controlling one's evil inclination. The Torah Says,
Genesis 4.7

וְאִם לֹא תֵיטִיב לַפֶּתַח חַטָּאת רֹבֵץ

And 'if' you do not do well, i.e if you do not improve yourself, sin Chah Tawt, meaning sin, חַטָּאת creeps at the door.

וְאֵלֶיךָ תְּשׁוּקָתוֹ וְאַתָּה תִּמְשָׁל־בּוֹ

It's desire is toward you, yet you can conquer it.

The Torah Portion of the Bible Teaches that we have power over the desires that bring about sin in each of our lives. Nothing is said about needing a redeemer or a savior. The Word וְאֵלֶיךָ Vih Ay Leh Chaw means 'to you or towards you'. The Word Vih Ah Taw means 'yet you...' The LORD is Teaching Cain that he has the ability to control his desires and to conquer his evil impulses. This is how we deal with issues. The LORD Gives each of us strength to conquer our desires. This is God's Plan and has ALWAYS been God's Plan.

Our Sages teach that Adam, the first man *After a period of time...* [spoke to his sons about offering sacrifices.] Genesis 3.3

Adam indicated that at this time in the future the upcoming date would be Passover. He explained to his sons that the Children of Israel would bring a Paschal sacrifice that would be favorably received by the Lord. Our sages state that in doing this he taught his sons, this is a propitious time for each of you to you bring a sacrifice to God, and He will be pleased with you... Rabbi Meir Zlotowitz and Rabbi Nosson Scherman, The Artscroll Tanach Series - Bereishis Vol. I(b) (Brooklyn, New York: Mesorah Publications, Ltd. 3rd Impression, 1989), p 144

Then, later, when Cain murdered his brother Abel

this put the entire world in a downward spiral. It was dark and depressing. The main point here is that it is easy to be like Cain. For example: Do we give the best of our morning hours to prayer? Is our Prayers offered in the prime time of the best of the afternoon? When do we say our evening hours to prayers? I understand. It is challenging to offer prayer at the best time in the morning, afternoon and evening. The issue is do we pray when it is convenient for us. How about May Ah Sar / tithing? Those that have the means, do we tithe? Do we pay the first fruits of our earnings? Do we pay the first fruits of our earnings before paying anything else? Look! These are two easy examples to offer on how we can be like Cain.

SUMMARY - There are many ways to give our Creator less than the best and from the back instead of the front so to speak. What do we do? Do we give from the best or the worst? What is the attitude of our heart? Do we desire to honor our Creator with the best or do we try to pawn off our junk and discards to our Creator?

Chapter Twelve

Offerings

Dear Ones, The Creator Provided a covering for Adam and Eve. They were naked. They needed a covering. The covering was not for their sin. The covering was for their nakedness. They were left bare after the Shekinah Presence withdrew from their outward beings. They repented of their sin. Our Creator took lamb's wool and goat hair braided with snake skin and made a special clothing for them to wear... Our Sages Teach that our Creator took these three items to design very special garments to cover and protect our first parents. The protection was very necessary because the animals who did not sin were now forced into a world of sin. All creation was angry with Adam and Eve. NOTHING at all is said about offering a animal sacrifice.

Taking life whether human or animal was forbidden until the year 1657 FC From Creation.

And God said [to Adam and Eve], Behold, I have given you every herb bearing seed, which is upon the face of all the earth, and every tree, on which is the fruit of a tree yielding seed; <u>to you it shall be for food,</u> Genesis 1.29.

[And God said] to every beast of the earth, and to every bird of the air, and to every thing that creeps upon the earth, where there is life, <u>I have given every green herb for food;</u> and it was so, Genesis 1.30.

The Lord God Did Not take the lives of animals to provide Adam and Eve / Chavah a covering.

Ha Torah Says,

וַיַּעַשׂ יְהוָה אֱלֹהִים לְאָדָם וּלְאִשְׁתּוֹ כָּתְנוֹת עוֹר וַיַּלְבִּשֵׁם :

Genesis 3.21
For Adam and for his wife the Lord God Made coats of **skins**, and clothed them.

The Word עוֹר ohr means, epidermis skins - meaning the outer layer. The serpent caused the problem so the Creator caused the Serpent to shed its outer layer skin. The Creator wove lamb / goats wool with skin from the serpent to form garments for Adam and Chavah. **There was no shedding of blood.**

Neither Cain nor Abel offered Animal Sacrifices.

וַיְהִי מִקֵּץ יָמִים וַיָּבֵא קַיִן מִפְּרִי הָאֲדָמָה מִנְחָה לַיהוָה:

Genesis 4.3.
And in process of time it came to pass, that Cain brought of the fruit of the ground an offering to the Lord.

This was spoiled flax seed. Cain's offering was not accepted because it was not from the first fruit and because the offering was spoiled flax seed. It was slimy. The Word מִנְחָה Minchah tells us the Offering was not meat. The offering was produce.

In Genesis 4.4 we review Abel's offering.

Genesis 4.4

וְהֶבֶל הֵבִיא גַם־הוּא מִבְּכֹרוֹת צֹאנוֹ וּמֵחֶלְבֵהֶן
וַיִּשַׁע יְהֹוָה אֶל־הֶבֶל וְאֶל־**מִנְחָתוֹ** :

And Abel also brought of the firstlings of his flock and of rich cream of it. And the Lord had respect for Abel and for his offering; One could also say rich cream or the fat of the offering because the spelling for rich cream and animal fat is the same. Yet we know it was not an animal offering because the Word **Minchato** tells us the Offering was not meat.

וַיִּבֶן נֹחַ מִזְבֵּחַ לַיהוָה וַיִּקַּח מִכֹּל
הַבְּהֵמָה הַטְּהֹרָה וּמִכֹּל הָעוֹף הַטָּהוֹר
וַיַּעַל עֹלֹת בַּמִּזְבֵּחַ:

Later Noach would bring a 'Burnt Offering'. This is identified by the Word עלת Oh Loht which represents it was a bird or animal. When the Word Minchah is used it is not an animal. When the Word Oh lam or Oh Loht are used it is an animal offering.

Abel's offering was accepted because it was from the 'first fruit'. The Offering came from a first born goat or lamb. We know this because of the Word מִבְּכֹרוֹת Mee Bih Coor Oht meaning 'from first born.' We know it was the best because of the Word וּמֵחֶלְבֵהֶן Oov May Cheh Lih Beh Hehn meaning 'And From the [rich] Cream. The offering was from the finest of the first born and the richest cream.

Dear Ones, if this discussion is upsetting to you I have an audio – <u>Offerings In The Bible</u> that maybe helpful. I explain how these misunderstandings may have begun. The misunderstandings come about from poor translations into English. It is understandable how English readers with little or no Hebrew language skills could become misled here.

Christians teach that when Adam and Eve sinned that they brought a blood offering. **NOT**

TRUE!

God Provided a skin covering from the wool of lamb and sheep woven with the shed skin of the serpent to clothe Adam and Chavah.   God Did Not Shed blood.

Christians also teach that the reason Cain's / Cain's offering was rejected was because it was not a blood offering.   Christians teach that the reason Abel's offering was accepted was because it was a blood offering. **NOT TRUE!**

Abel's Offering was noticed / accepted.   Cain's offering was NOT noticed / accepted. The Lord Gazes at Abel. Hashem does not Gaze towards Cain.   How should we define this?   Was this simply good fortune for Abel or was this something more? Was this happenstance, destiny or providence?   NO! It was not! Abel placed himself in a position that opened the doors of blessing. Cain did not.   It was not that good fortune just shined on Abel.   Abel did specific things that Cain did not do. This was the reason Hashem turned towards Abel. There were reasons why Hashem did not turn toward Cain. There were reasons why Hashem accepted Abel's Offering and not Cain's offering. Cain did specific things to cause Hashem to Turn away from him and his offering. Cain was a sinner.

1.) And he came, Cain, with fruit from the ground as an offering to Hashem... The ground was cursed because of Adam's sin, Genesis 3.17 [Bereisheit 3.17]. Cain brought fruit from the cursed ground, Genesis 4.3 [Bereisheit 4.3].

2.) Ha Torah Does not identify the ground from which the fruit was taken as belonging to Cain. Did Cain bring a stolen sacrifice?

3.) Midrash Tanchumah states, Cain's offering consisted of poor quality flax seed. *[Cain offered] inferior produce as a sacrifice, taking the best for himself. (Eitz Yosef}* Avrohom Davis, Metsudah Midrash Tanchuma Bereishis 1 (Monsey, NY Eastern Book Press Inc. 2005) p50

4.) Ha Torah Distinguishes from Cain's offering and Abel's offering. Cain's sacrifice was rejected because it was not of his first fruits. The flax seed that is brought was spoiled.

1.) Abel brought from his flocks.

2.) Abel brought from the firstborn of his flocks

3.) Abel brought the best from the first born of his flocks.

4.) Abel's offering was NOT A BLOOD SACRIFICE! The first sacrifice of animals or birds did not occur until 1657 F. C. in Genesis 8.20. It was at this time that our Creator began Allowing humankind to eat meat. Prior to 1657 F. C. every being was vegetarian. How do we know Abel did not offer a blood sacrifice? They did not build an altar because they were prohibited from slaughtering animals, (R' Yosief Kimchi; Tur). Rabbi Meir Zlotowitz and Rabbi Nosson Scherman, The Artscroll Tanach Series -

Bereishis Vol. I(a) (Brooklyn, New York: Mesorah Publications, Ltd. 3rd Impression, 1989), p 145

Abel kept his sheep chiefly for their wool (besides milk), for killing animals and eating them was forbidden... But why did the Torah say twice over, *'to Cain and to his offering and to Abel and to his offering?'* We can explain this on the basis of Chazal's comment that [God Did Not] Allow Adam to kill beasts or to consume their flesh. (He [Permitted] it only in Noah's time.) Rabbi Zalman Sorotzkin, Insights In The Torah - Bereishis (Brooklyn, NY: Mesorah Publications, Ltd. First Edition, 1991), p33

What was the Creator's Remedy for Cain's sin? The Creator's Remedy was to **IMPROVE YOURSELF**... If you conquer your temptation... If you do what's right you will be forgiven. Genesis 4.7

Christians teach that the only sacrifice for sin is a blood offering **NOT TRUE!**

Christians quote Hebrew 9:22, *But **ALMOST** all things are by the Law purged with blood and without the shedding of blood is no remission.* NOTE the word almost.

Christians teach that *It is not possible that the blood of bulls and of goats should take away sins.* New Writings Book Hebrews 10:4 **NOT TRUE!**

Stone Edition
Leviticus 5.11-13
But if his means are insufficient for two turtledoves or for two young doves, then he shall bring, as his guilt-offering for that which he sinned, a tenth-ephah of fine flour for a sin-offering; he shall not place oil on it nor shall he put frankincense on it, for it is a sin-offering. He shall bring it to the Priest, and the Priest shall scoop his three fingers full as its memorial portion and shall cause it to go up in smoke on the Altar, on the fires of The Lord; <u>it is a sin offering.</u> The Priest shall provide him atonement for the sin he

committed regarding any of these, and it will be forgiven him; and it shall belong to the Priest, like the meal-offering.

King James Version
Leviticus 5.11-13
But if he be not able to bring two turtledoves, or two young pigeons, then **he that sinned shall bring for his offering the tenth part of an ephah of fine flour for a sin offering;** he shall put no oil upon it, neither shall he put any frankincense thereon: for it is a sin offering. Then shall he bring it to the priest, and the priest shall take his handful of it, even a memorial thereof, and burn it on the altar, according to the offerings made by fire unto the LORD: **it is a sin offering. And the priest shall make an atonement for him as touching his sin that he hath sinned in one of these, and it shall be forgiven him:** and the remnant shall be the priest's, as a meat offering.

When man follows The Torah, The Torah atones for man. How do we know this? The Gematrias are the same. The Torah is Perfect. The Torah can and does atone for man. So in the Observance of Torah we see the portrayal of atonement for man.

Unfortunately there are those who have allowed themselves to be misled by our Jewish affectionate use of referring to God as our Father. Our intent was NEVER to imply that God had a son. We recognize that it is IMPOSSIBLE for God to have a son.

However this is understandable to us. Our Creator chooses to Reveal Himself differently between various groups. Remember what our Creator Said,

Exodus 6.4
And [I] Appeared to Avraham, to Isaac and to Jacob as God Almighty and not by My Name The Lord. [I] did not reveal to them.

No matter how much we teach and share that God is ONLY ONE, some will not receive it because God has not revealed it to them. They are following God with the light He has provided them. So no matter how much I want others to understand that God is Not three in One, until the Creator reveals this to them, they will not understand.

I invite you to join class discussions on this subject at bnti.us. Look for *Would you like to be Jewish*? Click on the link.

Review other books by Dr. Akiva Gamliel Belk at: bnti.us/books.html

ABOUT THE AUTHOR

Dr. Akiva Gamliel Belk

Jewish, Husband, Father, Grandfather and Step Great Grandfather.

Graduate:
A.A. Long Beach City College,
B.A. Southern California Bible College,
M.A. Southern California Theological Seminary,
D. Th. Southern California Theological Seminary,
D. Th. Denver Charismatic Theological Seminary

Individual Study:
Rabbi Dovid Nusbaum,
Bais Medrash at Yeshiva Toras Chaim,
Hornosteipler Rebbe, Mordicai Tewerski

Group Study:
Rabbi Yaakov Meyer, Aish Denver
Rabbi Israel Engel, Director, Colorado Chabad.

Founder:
Jewishpath.org
Jewishlink.net
7commands.com
Buntings

Dean of Jewish Studies
B'nai Noach Torah Institute, LLC – Biblical Online Studies

Author of various books.
bnti.us/books.html

Businessman:
Realtor and Property Investor

www.ingramcontent.com/pod-product-compliance
Lightning Source LLC
LaVergne TN
LVHW051837080426
835512LV00018B/2935